The Science of Story Selling:

How to **Win the Hearts & Minds** of Your Prospects for **Profit and Purpose**

Gideon F. For-mukwai

ISBN: Softcover 978-981-09-5103-0

For further information visit www.ScienceOfStorySellingforProfit.com

FOREWORD

Having been a professional speaker for several decades, I know the importance of business storytelling as a powerful vehicle for conveying ideas and messages to my audiences and clients in over 100 countries.

A good story can make or break a presentation or business opportunity. In my experience, it has enabled me to persuade thousands of followers and subscribers worldwide.

These days, we are literally submerged by too much information. Unfortunately, data or information without context cannot enable us to live safe and happy lives. We need storytelling and narratives to give us perspectives that are more understandable and useful in every day life.

To navigate through life, we all need good storytellers that will provide the inspiration and interpretations of the trends in business and new opportunities. Entrepreneurs, trainers, speakers, and coaches ought to be master storytellers because they are bearers of the truth. They must inform, inspire and influence customers. Above all, if you want to make a living, you need to understand persuasion. A large part of persuasion, copywriting and sales is storytelling.

If you are serious about developing yourself or growing your business, you need to pay a close attention to business storytelling. It could mean the difference between earning big bucks from sales, or being down and broke.

Tom Antion

Founder Great Internet Marketing Retreat Center and Joint Venture Program

http://www.GreatInternetMarketingTraining.com

Praise for *The Science of Story Selling*

I find Gideon's book fascinating to read. It's a must read for every salesperson, politician, and clergyman, but especially parents and teachers. I make living telling stories, and I'm one of the few storytelling comedians alive today. I grew up listening to comedians on the radio, and they were magnificent storytellers who knew how to build a story that would have several laughs and then the payoff. Congratulations on a great idea.

~Tom Dreesen, American Standup Comedian and Philanthropist, Chicago, USA

I find your ideas and style refreshing for worldwide audiences. I believe that they will revolutionize how stories impact public speaking and other related disciplines.

~Dr. Khumbulani D. Mdletshe, Author and Educator, Johannesburg, South Africa

Wow! You've penned a terrific book. I've read a number of works in the same genre, most recently "The Dragonfly Effect" and "Made to Stick," and would put yours right there with them as enormously helpful guides, not just for business people, but for all people wanting their call to action to be heard. In a world overflowing with messages of every sort flowing on seemingly every wavelength simultaneously, getting yours heard can be daunting. Master storyteller Gideon F. For-mukwai makes it much less so with this indispensable guide chock-full of example-backed strategies that ensure your call to action captures the attention of your intended audience. Though penned for business people, this book offers everyone power tools for effective communication and skillful persuasion.

~Scott Dogett, Veteran Journalist, Writer/Editor Los Angeles Times, USA

How do brands portray their brand experience? By telling a story. A story of the experience behind the brand, a story narrated in short ad films like: Pantene and its shampoo adverts, Apple in the famous Misfits ad, KFC and the famous story of Colonel Sanders and how he got started. Without a story, the product is just that—a product—without a life. A story brings the product to life, thus attracting a tribe that represents the product story and brand mission. It's a powerful client attraction & brand loyalty strategy.

~Suria Mohd, Founder iMentor Training Academy, Singapore

In this simple, yet informative and eye-opening book, Gideon F. For-mukwai builds on Chinua Achebe's belief that "The story is our escort; without it, we are blind." The author painstakingly lays out the steps for transforming a story – a mere literary art form – into a formidable scientific tool for winning clients, building brands and inspiring audiences.

~Dibussi Tande, Cameroonian Poet,
Award Winning Blogger,
Journalist, Writer, Chicago, USA

At once deeply theoretical and intensely practical, *The Science of Story-Selling* is a must-read for anyone who earns a living by speaking in front of others. Beginning with insights from recent neuroscience research that our brain responds to specific words and phrases, Gideon F. For-mukwai, drawing upon a wealth of personal experience, shares powerful tools, techniques and strategies that will allow you to engage your customers with stories. In essence, "stories are the lifeblood of any presentation," and just imagine using the simple but profound techniques of *Story-Selling* to uplift and inspire those you speak to, and how that ability can transform your businesses or career.

~Michael Edward Lenert, J.D., Ph.D.,
Attorney at Law, Professor of Media Studies,
the University of San Francisco

Stories are an integral part of my strategy and my business arsenal. I recommend this book for any business owner working on a shoestring budget. This will help you take charge and win more associates, prospects and customers.

~Fadilah Majid, Former Business Editor
Beritan Harian, Singapore,
Managing Director, Spa Jelita

As a business author and trainer, I have seen the positive impact of connecting emotionally with your prospects and clients. There is no better way than making this connection through effective story telling. Mr. For-mukwai has done an outstanding job explaining and teaching this very valuable concept.

~Nikkos Zorbas, Author:
Discover Your Business Power,
Las Vegas, Nevada, USA

I've applied some of the storytelling concepts in this book to my signature story. I am confident to say, it has made my story more memorable to participants at my sold-out business boot camps. I highly recommend this book for entrepreneurs who want to be more engaging, remarkable and memorable.

~Imran Md Ali,
Founder of the Profit Academy,
Singapore

In this easy-to-read, very practical book, Gideon For-mukwai successfully marries the art and science of story telling in a compelling and refreshing way. The useful tips and the 30-day challenge would make a novice a believer. Whether you are an independent consultant, a teacher, or a business professional who wishes to directly engage your audience to achieve whatever your objectives may be, this book is a must read!

~Dr. Amiso M. George, APR, Fellow PRSA,
Assoc. Professor of Strategic Communication,
Texas Christian University, USA

When we look back at our lives, we realize that we have been moulded more by stories than anything else. Big stories, little stories, serious stories, funny stories. How often we come away so happy from a party or a movie because we heard a good story. And then we played it back in our minds again and again. We might forget the narrator, but we do not forget a good story. I believe Gideon's storytelling approach in this book is worth very careful study.

Sahana Singh, Editor,
Asian Water Magazine

This book discusses principles that I have used over and over in my business. The person with a better story wins the heart and minds of the customer. I have used this idea to boost my business from zero. This explains why I like the idea of "Your Story is Your Asset," expressed in this book.

~AbangAbu Abuaybul Ansari,
Founder of Highway to Wealth,
Singapore - Malaysia

A primary objective when communicating with an audience is ensuring that the subject, whether mundane or forlorn, can be easily grasped. More often than not, an audience will be more engaged when a theme is seen to be specifically relevant to them. To do that, I often use stories to drive the point home. This book offers numerous ideas you can use to make the complex easier to grasp.

~Abah Ofon, Financial Markets Consultant,
London, United Kingdom

As Senior Policy Analyst, Software Engineer and Healthcare Administrator of some of the World Harvard Teaching Hospitals, very often I have to use narratives and compelling stories to engage my audiences on a variety of complex assignments. "The Science of Story Selling" offers new ideas and concepts from a neuroscientist's perspective. I believe every effective leader with a need to deconstruct complex issues using compelling narratives will draw insights from this book. This young writer will transform your ability to communicate effectively with non-specialists. If you are in a position to lead, here comes a must-read from Mr. For-mukwai – a book you cannot ignore.

Dr. Agwo Tata,
Beth Israel Deaconess Medical Center,
Harvard Medical School Teaching Hospital

Thank goodness Gideon F. For-mukwai has written a book about the power of storytelling. He is a master storyteller and shares his wisdom with us here. The most important moments of my personal and professional life are related to stories, or are best told as stories.

~Meggin McIntosh, Ph.D.,
Productivity Coach, Reno, Nevada

Acknowledgements

In Africa we say it takes a village to build a hut, however small. I am grateful that my village is bigger, better, smarter than I am. Each time I needed help while working on this book, my fellow global villagers pitched in.

Without the literary and editorial help of Ms. Barbara Lauger of the USA, this "hut" would be incomplete.

I am grateful to my family and friends, Eden Neba of Sacramento California, Timothy Tembon of Johannesburg, South Africa, and Agherenwi Neba of London.

To me, intelligence is not enough. I've often leaned on the wise counsel of Mr. Nathaniel Forbes of Minnesota, USA. He is made from a special fiber—a fiber that our world so desperately needs. Such is also the case of Dr. Nicoline Ambe of Los Angeles, California, whose work ethic is mind-blowing.

In Singapore, I am most grateful to Kaixin Akwi and Melissa Lee for their graphic-selection acumen. To my business associates Timothy Ong and Badrulhisham, you guys have helped me fight some invisible fires you couldn't see. Your authenticity inspires me!

In several ways, I owe a big kudos to my friend Imran Md Ali, a marketing genius par excellence for his ideas regarding the book title and focus. What a friend! Last but not least, I am most grateful to Diana M. Needham for her executive oversight and relentless quality control acumen.

It's a pity I can't mention every villager's name. You are my unsung heroes; you come from a lineage of kings, warriors and gladiators. Yours is a lineage that I will forever honor. Yes, I will. I'll shine the light to others, as you have done for me. To you all, I say IOU! *Mbene wen moh! Xie-xie, Merci, Danke!*

Dedication

To a widow and warrior,
A woman who couldn't read or write her name,
But whose love lights up my path.
Her love for work and work for love
Had no measure or censure
But lots to be treasured
For enduring my troubled youth,
With bruises and burns from all the fires I lit,
And the taunts from the mockingbirds
That I'd be a jailbird.
Instead, her love nurtured me to be a thunderbird,
Bringing rain to the crops and the birds.
To my mother, my hero - **Catherine Akwi [RIP]**

Special Bonus from Gideon

Now that you have your copy of **The Science of Story Selling**, you are on your way to telling breathtaking stories! Remember this; your stories are like an invisible musical instrument that you can use to win the hearts and minds of your prospects for profit or a purpose.

You'll also receive a **special bonus** I've created for you. It is what I call *Hollywood Storytelling Secrets for Business Professionals*. It is a study of the key lessons that iconic Hollywood story masters teach their clients. Hopefully, their ideas will inspire you to tell remarkable and memorable stories.

Do you want your stories to be indelible in the minds of your audiences? Start right here.

While *Hollywood Storytelling Secrets* is offered for sale, as a special bonus you can claim it for **free** here:

http://scienceofstorysellingforprofit.com/bookbonus/

The sooner you master these secrets, the better your chances for gaining more likeability and credibility that potentially leads to more profitability.

Let me know if I can be of further help.

Remember: When there is no connection, there is no persuasion,

Gideon F. For-mukwai

TABLE OF CONTENTS

Why I Became Obsessed With Business Storytelling

Have you ever given a presentation you wish you could take back?

Have you ever made a business pitch you wished you could redo?

I've had my fair share of both. One case stands out. In 2005, I gave a presentation in Toronto, Canada that made me feel so bad about my future career and myself. In retrospect, if I'd been paid for that gig, I'd have returned the check.

Barely five minutes into my presentation, I started slowly on a journey of self-destruction and implosion with my PowerPoint slides. I stuttered, stammered and struggled to pronounce words. My mouth was dry, but I didn't have the courage to ask for water. It was a dreadful day!

As I wandered around the stage like a chimp in a cage, I thought of just running out through the door to get lost. It felt like I was locked up in a deep, dark basement with no windows. I was insecure about myself, especially speaking to a native English-speaking audience for the first time. I thought they were judging my modest English. The problem indeed, was not the audience. I'd designed my death with my PowerPoint, and I left no room for a personal connection or resurrection.

When it was all over, I felt so bad about myself. People often ask me, how bad was it? I tell them, it was so bad that even the coffee lady didn't want to make eye contact with me. Ouch!

A few weeks later, I did a post-mortem of the Toronto tragedy. I figured I needed a speaking coach, and I contacted Jean Gatz, CSP in the USA. In recounting the Toronto nightmare to her, she found out that my presentation was entirely loaded with mountains and mountains of data and facts. It was void of any stories of my views, or of me. I kept justifying to her, "It was a technical presentation."

After a long pause, I recall Jean telling me, *"Gideon, stories are the lifeblood of a presentation, however technical."*

For a few months, she taught me some powerful tools, techniques and strategies on how to better engage with stories. What I learned from her has changed my style of presenting, and business as a whole. She taught me how to infuse stories with interest, to be conversational, and to deliver a message that leaves imprints on the hearts and minds of the audience.

Fortunately for me, in November that year, I had an opportunity to redo the Toronto presentation in Phoenix, Arizona, for another group. Thanks to Jean's coaching, it was a very different outcome for me. It was a far cry from the Toronto meltdown. It was not necessarily a great presentation, but coming from the ruins of Toronto, I thought I had a field day. I'm sure if the Toronto coffee lady were there, she'd not have avoided making eye contact with me again. Perhaps she might have winked at me.

The Phoenix resurrection taught me a very important lesson. It taught me that effective stories can transform technical presentations from arid and dead to alive and exhilarating. It also taught me that, "What trips in Canada, takes off in America."

But for the changes, Phoenix could've been another Toronto trial. Or worse, it could have been my Waterloo. But it turned out to be my Sputnik moment. It awakened me to the bitter realities of growing my career beyond the confines of one country or region.

Four years after the Phoenix presentation, I met a gentleman in Reno, Nevada. He was one of a few hundred who'd taken part in the Phoenix talk. I obviously had no memory of him at all. After several meetings at his office, he asked me a question that changed my fortunes that summer of 2009.

"Are you the guy who once presented at the IAEM Conference in Phoenix in 2005?"

"Yes," I responded.

"Are you the one who told us about avian flu in Asia?"

"Yes, sir"

"Ahhh, I remember you! You told us a story about a farmer in Vietnam who got infected by a chicken?"

That was a rare moment! How often do you meet someone who remembers you and your story after four years? In my mind I was saying, "God forbid him from asking me to retell that story. I couldn't do justice to that story with as much detail as Mr. Kenneston was about to flesh it out.

In retrospect, I know that moment would not have been possible, but for the skills Jean Gatz gave me. Here is the icing on the cake, for you cake lovers. Thanks to that warm and positive memory, Mr. Kenneston said, "Am glad to know you've been around the block doing good work." To top it off, he doubled my hourly internship stipend from $23 to $43/hour! For a year as tough as 2009, I couldn't have been more grateful. Finding graduate internships was very tough. Getting one that had a stipend was even harder, not just for foreign students like me, but also for American students with godfathers around the block.

For me, it was just surreal and unprecedented to have such a windfall, thanks to a story I told four years earlier. I invite you to stick with me because I went from studying with Jean Gatz to several other masters of the game. I've studied under Patricia Fripp, CSP, CPAE, and World Champion Speakers such as Darren LaCroix, Craig Valentine, and Ed Tate.

Twice I drove 16 hours, and sometimes through desert hailstorms in Mesquite, Nevada, to take classes from Ms. Fripp and Mr. Darren LaCroix. On one occasion, I got a traffic ticket at midnight. My friends ask me, was it worth it? I tell them, without a shadow of doubt. This one skill has changed my fortunes and my life. If there is just one thing I must share with you on this terrestrial journey, it must be the skill of Storytelling.

It has also taken me to over 18 countries, none of which I had to pay a dime to travel to. Not bad for kid who had to wait 26 years to fly for the first time. This skill has earned many opportunities and awards that I can't elaborate about here.

Recently, I started dabbling at coaching others on how to use this skill to transform their businesses as Story Warriors who work relentlessly to win the hearts and minds of their customers. So far, so good.

Some of my trainees are using their new skills to build their brands, get more attention from students in class, prospects in the marketplace, run campaigns to generate leads and engage customers, gain more customer advocates, and deepen their sales connections and conversions.

My obsession for this subject has also led me to discover that there is a science that underlies the art. This is where my approach is distinctly different from the rest. This is where I seek to say that all storytellers are not born equal. May I confide in you? I believe you and I can combine the science and the art of storytelling to create a bit of magic that no other master crafter out there is talking about right now.

In a crowded marketplace where people have attention spans as low as that of a gold fish, we badly need storytelling to capture and hold their attention. Attention by itself is a new currency, and the story is the gold standard.

Imagine what it will mean to your business if you are able to identify which neurons you need to stimulate to get better attention and resonance in pitching your product or service. It is time to know why stories sell, while others repel. Imagine the implications of this knowledge on your business. Imagine using this for good causes to boost your reputation and brand in the marketplace.

Here is all I can say for now: the Science of Story-Selling can change your business forever. It can also help you to be a better human being, who touches the hearts and minds of people for a purpose bigger than profit.

Permit me to ask you just one question: If this story thing is unlocking new doors for a country bumpkin from Africa, how much more for you?

Thanks for investing your time to find out.

Why the Science of Story-Selling Today?

World-famous screen writing instructor, Robert McKee, says, "Storytelling is the most powerful way to put ideas into the world today."

Do you know you can use your stories as an invisible instrument to tug away at your audience's heartstrings? In the process of doing this, you can teach, influence, and inspire others to be nicer and happier. By doing so, you build likability, affinity, credibility, and trust.

In today's world, likability, affinity, and credibility are assets. These assets are worth investing in. They will differentiate you from your competitors. If you want to engage and persuade your audience, this is where you must start. Persuasion is an art. Coercion won't work. Gun toting won't work!

If you want to move your audience persuasively, and not coercively, then storytelling is for you. A well-told story is an asset that yields dividends. Here is the good news: it is not taxable! This is one asset that the taxman has ignored for thousands of years. Learn to milk this cash cow while it lasts.

So why do I say your story is an asset? Think of it this way, a well-told story has a return on investment (ROI). It helps you earn the following benefits short term and long term:

Attention-getter

There is no better attention-getter. Not your Ivy League education. Not your family name. If you can tell a good story, you'll be in demand. People will talk about you, and this will create a positive buzz. Always. You can take this idea to the bank. I've seen this in Asia, Africa, Europe and America.

Seed-sower

In a world with indescribable persuasive pressures, storytelling is a refreshing, noninvasive form of persuasion that quietly sows ideas in the mind of the listener or reader. It's gentle, interesting, and yet most persuasive.

Stimulate action

A well-told story has the potential to galvanize action. It is like a catalyst. Do you think Americans would have marched if Martin Luther King, Jr. appeared on stage to read a litany of facts, or with a PowerPoint? He moved his audience with compelling stories.

Emo-du-tain

This is one aspect of storytelling that everyone likes, but few can deliberately embed into their speeches or scripts. Emodutainment has to do with emotional engagement, educational involvement and entertainment. This happens when a story is touching, moving, and yet funny. My professional hero, Mr. Tom Dreesen, is great at this craft. He used to tour with Frank Sinatra. Mr. Dreesen is a tireless comedian, philanthropist and master storyteller. He is capable of making you learn, laugh, and cry, all at the same time.

Trust-builder

Stories allow us to be vulnerable and human without being despicable. They enable us to connect intellectually and emotionally with others, thereby leaning on their humanity and earning their trust and confidence.

Thus, in essence, our stories get us attention and recognition. With attention, you can use carefully selected characters to sow seeds of interest, and spark action in the minds of your audience. Let your characters emotionally engage, educate and entertain them for you. This is one of the most cost-effective ways of building trust in today's attention-deficit times.

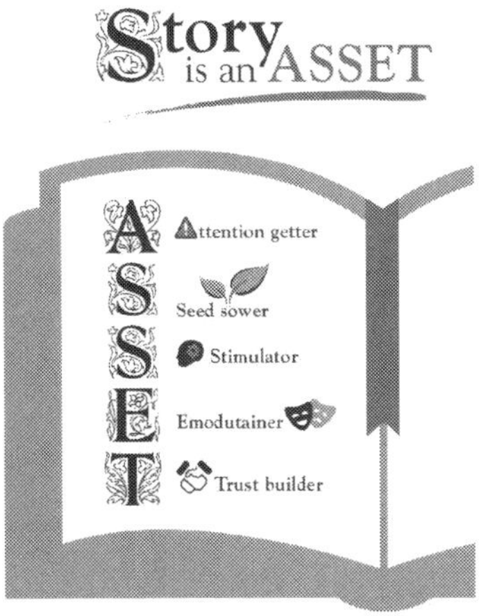
Story is an ASSET
A Attention getter
S Seed sower
S Stimulator
E Emodutainer
T Trust builder

PART 1

Understand the Underlying Science That Makes Storytelling the Best Way to Win the Hearts and Minds of Your Audience Today

Chapter 1:

The Underlying Science of Storytelling - Why it Works Like Magic

Section 1: What Happens in the Brain When a Story is Being Told

"A story is the only way to activate the brain so that listeners turn the story into their own idea and experience. Storytelling is the only way to plant ideas into other people's minds."

~ Uri Hasson, Researcher, University of Princeton.

Have you ever been moved to act a certain way after listening to a story? Have you ever donated money or participated in a cause, thanks to a compelling story that outlined the benefits of your contribution?

To a large extent, I believe your answer is, "Yes." Like you, I have contributed numerous times to different causes. Sometimes, I have voted for candidates based on their stories.

The reason well-told stories get us to think or act is that we are naturally hardwired for stories. Stories have the ability to alter our brain chemistry—neurons, hormones, blood pressure, etc.

If you are a teacher, entrepreneur or leader, chances are you give presentations to small or large groups. Have you ever wondered which is more effective in audience engagement and why—a PowerPoint presentation, or a narrative presentation?

PowerPoint vs. Story-Point Dilemma

What if Martin Luther King, Jr. had given the "I Have a Dream" speech with PowerPoint slides? I have also wondered what would have happened if Winston Churchill had given his now-famous "Never Give Up" speech with PowerPoint slides.

Which is better: the PowerPoint or a **story** point? Both are useful. Both can be insightful; however, when it comes to persuasion, telling a compelling story has greater potency. Let's explore some of the science underlying this.

Thanks to functional magnetic resonance imaging (fMRI) studies, it is now known that the chemistry of the brain changes significantly during an engaging story. This is particularly true "when you listen to an emotionally-charged story," according to Dr. Paul Zak, a pioneer in the field of neuro-economics.

When you deliver a PowerPoint presentation, the outcome in terms of brain chemistry is different from when you tell an engaging story. Both are similar, but have very different outcomes. It is as though one is from Jupiter, and the other from Siberia. When listening to a story, both the left and right sides of the brain are engaged. They come alive. This is a far cry from what happens when a hotshot MBA holder delivers a PowerPoint presentation that is full of complex charts, graphs, and statistics that only engage the left brain.

Stories tend to be more engaging in that they are relatable and arouse feelings. Take, for instance, the fact that you mention in your story that you took a warm bath with a lavender-scented soap. This elicits a sensual response beyond the language-processing areas of our brains that tends to be focused on facts, figures, and logic. Thus, a story that is carefully crafted gives you greater room to embed sensory language that stimulates the brain to imagine new realities. Good storytellers use words to paint pictures, because some words have a great emotional impact on the brain. Some words arouse. Some words depress and some words uplift. In some cultures, the N-word depresses. It could even stir strong emotions instantly. This shows that by using a story, you have greater latitude to engage, and move your audience forward.

PowerPoint presentations tend to activate the **Broca's** and **Wernicke's** area of the brain. These areas are primarily responsible for language processing, i.e., where we decode words into meaning. If you are the creator of Rosetta Stone language home study, that is good news for you.

There is nothing wrong with that, if the sole focus of your presentation is to share facts. If, on the other hand, you want to persuade, presenting facts alone will not be sufficient. It would get the desired goal, just like you can't cut down a tree with chopsticks. Is that enough?

On the other hand, if you are a director or business owner, and you strive to be more engaging, activating only the predominantly left brain logic part of your brain is not sufficient in persuading or inspiring a prospect to go online and download your white paper or e-book.

Why it is Important to Understand How Stories Affect Your Brain

You are the captain of your ship. You don't want it to sink, do you? As the captain of your ship, I believe you want to do all it takes to keep sailing. This means the more you know about the dynamics of water, weather, and your ship, the better your sailing at sea. Having a mastery of how your brain receives and digests stories will put you in a stronger position as the captain who knows how to pilot the ship in safe and stormy waters.

This can make or break your style of engagement. Whether as a teacher, entrepreneur or a leader, you are in the business of not only informing, but inspiring, and influencing people to do the things they would otherwise procrastinate doing.

Thus, your understanding of the way the brain works allows you to know you have the possibility of engaging both the left and right hemispheres of the brain, or whole brain, as some authors prefer to call it. Whole brain is definitely better than half brain.

To do that job, you can use stories. Stories stimulate the brain better. By telling someone about a delicious meal you ate at a French restaurant, the listener's sensory cortex is activated (lights up) i.e., the same areas of pleasure, as though he were enjoying the real meal.

By talking about a fantastic joy ride through a downtown area on a world-class motorbike, the listener's motor cortex brain lights up. This type of brain activation goes beyond the left brain. It extends to the right brain that controls emotions; hence, an opportunity for you to inspire or influence. PowerPoint works like chocolate, while stories stimulate like a double shot of espresso coffee. In real life, the difference can be poignant. It could mean someone holding tight to his or her wallet, or opening it to make a donation to your project or cause.

Section 2: Getting Past the Amygdala, or the Gatekeeper

The amygdala is a pair of almond-shaped structures (mass of nuclei) in the limbic brain. It processes emotions and aggression for the "fight or flight" decisions. It controls fear responses, the secretion of hormones, arousal, and formation of emotional memories. Researchers have found that the amygdala plays an important role in emotional learning.

Thus, if you share information with people or groups, it is important to understand how to get the amygdala's attention and collaboration in memory formation. Ideally, you should choose stories and words that have emotional undertones to be able to get the amygdala's attention, i.e., in the minds of your audience.

By doing so, you not only employ but deploy the amygdala in the spread of ideas and messages, because it is connected to all parts of the brain, and also controls secretions of neurons and hormones. By taking advantage of your knowledge of the workings of the brain in general, and the amygdala in particular, you can source, craft, and deliver stories that leave a lasting impact on the brain.

When choosing characters, scenes, or messages, remember that the amygdala modulates the rhythm of the brain with respect to what is important, safe, unsafe, scary, not scary, bland, frightening, exciting, dull, etc. Based on this understanding, you can craft stories with messages that leverage its sensitivities to the fight-or-flight mechanism. In other words, a character with scary features is more memorable and attention getting than a plain Jane. Just remember that once things get emotional, like during an earthquake, domestic violence, car accident, fall from a tree, or just simple crashing or slamming of the door, this will cause the amygdala to kick in stronger.

Studies have shown that a slight emotional arousal right after you learn something can increase memory. This can be simulated or stimulated naturally, through the use of an engaging story that causes a greater secretion of adrenaline by the adrenal glands.

For instance, a fairly graphic story of a mother who watches her son be struck by a car. The son is injured, and has many fractured bones in his right leg. Within days, his leg is amputated, and then in a feat of luck, is asked by a new doctor to come back in for the amputated leg to be sewed back on. The audience will go through a swing of emotions as the amygdala goes from pain and misery, to hope and action.

In the above example, the amygdala plays a powerful role in the way the brain functions. It can even highjack the brain during an emergency, i.e., superseding other functions when it senses a threat to survival or eminent danger.

Want Your Story to be Memorable? Learn How to Stimulate the Amygdala

The amygdala is responsible for encoding and the storage of hippocampal (the part of the brain that looks like a sea horse), or long-term memories. It is particularly good at emotion-based (fear) memory formation. Beware of the fact that, an over-stimulation can be counter-productive.

Several studies have demonstrated that emotion can influence attention, by both capturing it, and altering the ease with which emotional stimuli are processed when attention is limited. Although most of the research examining amygdala— hippocampal interaction has explored how the amygdala can influence episodic (autobiographical, time, place, who, what, where and when) memory, there is also evidence of episodic memory influencing the amygdala.

In a typical fear-conditioning situation, a subject learns how a stimulus predicts an adverse event by virtue of its pairing. In everyday human experience, this type of learning often occurs. For example, if a neighbor's dog bit you, the next time you encounter this dog, you might have a fear response. This is an everyday example of fear conditioning.

However, for humans it is also possible to learn about the emotional significance of stimuli in the environment through other means, such as verbal communication. You might have a similar fear response to the neighborhood's dog if your neighbor had previously told you that it was a dangerous dog that might bite you if you attempted to trespass in search of his pretty daughter.

This type of learning through instruction requires the hippocampal complex for acquisition, and possibly for retrieval, when the fearful stimulus is present. Through instruction, subjects can acquire an episodic representation of the emotional significance of an event without any direct aversive experience.

The question is, does this hippocampal-dependent episodic representation of emotion influence the amygdala? In an fMRI study, subjects were told that they would receive one or more mild shocks to the wrist, but only when a blue square was presented. Although no shocks were actually presented, subjects showed an arousal response during presentation of the blue square, as well as activation of the left amygdala. A similar study found that damage to the left amygdala impaired the physiological fear response to the blue square.

These results suggest that having an instructed, episodic representation of the emotional significance of a stimulus can lead to activation of the amygdala. Given amygdala's role in processing or mediating the physiological expression of fear when the stimulus is encountered, this implies that a fictional story can equally engage and arouse neural and hormonal activation. This can result in imagined or anticipated fears or excitement. Therefore, such neural mechanisms appear to be as real as those learned or based on direct experience.

Thus, if you are a teacher, entrepreneur, or leader, you can take advantage of this, thereby engaging your followers with fictional stories that help them feel the transformation you want them to experience. This is what marketers have been doing for decades now. They use evocative and often fictional stories to nudge us to buy their products or take the next action.

What Does This Mean for Professionals Who Regularly Interact With Audiences?

When outlining your speaking, teaching or empowerment ideas to engage an audience include stories. Not only will this make you more approachable, it will also make you more memorable. Your stories will serve as the vehicle through which to illustrate and convey your message to your audience. In other words, stories lubricate and anchor your ideas in the minds of your audience. To better engage and earn the attention of your audience, start with an idea steeped in unease or trepidation. When this happens, the ultrasensitive gatekeeper to the brain, the amygdala, tunes in.

This means there is focus or attention. With this window of opportunity, you must leverage it to sow important seeds and transition quickly to another activity, key point, or story that releases the tension. An interesting, humorous or happy ending will cut it better, at this point.

It allows you to give the audience something of pleasure: a smile, giggle, a chuckle, or something of pleasure for enduring the earlier story that was laced with some anxiety.

By weaving anxious with uplifting, pain with gain, darkness with light, and evil with virtuous moments, you enable the brain to be engaged. During a moment of accomplishment and excitement, the brain secretes dopamine, the reward chemical of the brain, or oxytocin, the care, empathy and bonding chemical or hormone.

Theory of the Mind, the Insular Cortex, & How We Make Sense of Life through Stories

Each time you hear a story, the insular cortex comes alive. It is a part of your brain that helps you relate to another person's situation, without experiencing their pain, fear, disgust, or joy. It gives you the ability to have a better understanding of his or her state of emotions, and the complexities of the situation, without having to be in the same shoes. This is one of the things that make us deeply human. This helps you make sense of our complex world, hence helping to develop your own self-awareness.

Without this ability, we'd be incapable of learning from the mistakes our friends or parents made few weeks back. In other words, we'd more error-prone. This can be costly! Thanks to this function of the brain, you are able to learn from their mistakes, concerns or, aspirations, prejudices that are expressed through daily conversations and stories.

"A story is the only way to activate the brain so that listeners turn the story into their own idea and experience. Storytelling is the only way to plant ideas into other people's minds."

~Uri Hasson, Researcher, University of Princeton.

Section 3: Put Neurons to Work in Your Stories to Stir Up Desirable Action(s)

For years, I thought storytelling was purely an art. In the last three years, I found out that I was wrong. Emerging research from neuroscience tells me there is a solid rock of science on which the stories stand. Those who know how to reach that rock, and move or cause it to fizzle or result in effervescence in the mind, are able to accomplish more.

Plato once said, "Those who tell stories rule society."

Through the choice of your words, idioms, anecdotes, and metaphors, the imagery and literary devices that you use to engage your listeners or audience, you get to reach that massive "rock" of neurons and hormones that are capable of stirring things up in human emotions. Whether overtly or covertly, the better you are at creating a stronger mixing of the chemicals in the brain and bloodstream, the better your storytelling will be.

By this I mean that your understanding of how the neurons and hormones are stimulated can go a long way in helping to craft better stories artistically. An effective understanding of these chemicals enables you to draw the audience into your world, literally and neurologically.

Here some of the neurons you need to be aware of that impact on your listeners as you tell your stories. By amplifying some elements of your story, you are capable of taking your audience into a fantasy that rules or captivates the mind. Just as moviemakers are capable of making you happy, sad, and sometimes misty-eyed with the power of their stories, you are capable of selecting and telling stories that can defy the physical. Thanks to a phenomenon known as neural coupling, you can get the listener's brain to "dance the same dance" as you, the teller.

Neural Coupling

This occurs when there is verbal communication. Through the use of fMRI, it is now understood that brain activity of listeners reflects that of speakers or the storyteller during verbal or oral communication.

The speaker's activity is spatially and temporally coupled with the listener's activity. This coupling vanishes when communication or storytelling stops. In a room full of people, the socially dominant person sets the tone. You can put this understanding to good use by carefully selecting what you want your audience to experience when you tell your story. Do you want it to be slow, fast, exhilarating, or fascinating? The choice is yours. "You have the knife and the yam," as they say in Africa.

1. Mirror Neurons:

These neurons are fired in the brain when an action is performed, or when you observe another person performing an action. When a storyteller shares a moving or dreadful experience, both the brain of the teller and the listener undergo similar neurochemical changes. Here are areas where you can get your audience to be fully engaged: describe movements, speak with the feet or hands, or talk about food with strong flavor, such as freshly baked cookies or cinnamon. This awareness enables you sharpen your ability to craft more engaging and compelling stories that connect you deeper with your audience.

2. Cortisol

This hormone is also known as the stress-inducing hormone. It is often associated with distress. It however, it has a positive side. It enables you and your audience to focus when an issue of high significance such as the health impact of diabetes or heart disease is being shared. By increasing our attention and focus, both storyteller and the audience benefit.

By choosing a topic that affects an audience's health, financial, emotional, or spiritual well-being, a presenter or speaker invariably increases his or her chances of getting greater attention. To increase of deepen their attention; the speaker or storyteller can introduce elements of urgency or uncertainty. The amygdala i.e. the "gatekeeper" pays particular attention to such issues and conveys their urgency to the rest of the brain. When a stressful story is being told, the hormone is secreted, enabling the listener to pay much closer attention or focus.

Greater attention is a good asset to have these days when most people are often distracted by technology. It therefore, provides a better opportunity for effective communication, persuasion or motivation. You can put your understanding of this chemical to good use by choosing and crafting stories strategically to increase your audience‘s attention when required to make an important point.

My understanding of this hormone has enabled me to choose attention-getting stories at the start of my presentations. Once I have the undivided attention of the audience, I can then leverage it to teach important lessons. Do not abuse your understanding of this hormone in your speaking, because audiences can suffer stress fatigue.

3. Oxytocin

Oxytocin is referred to as a bonding or intimacy chemical. It supports or encourages empathy, connections and compassion for one another. If a story is void of subtle and moving parts that show connectedness or lack of, it leaves much to be desired. You can't afford to ignore the power of oxytocin in your stories.

A little more of this hormone will allow the audience to be drawn into the scene, toward the issues at stake. A story that describes a baby whose mother is sick and injured, willing to breastfeed but unable to do so, will physically get the audience's attention and yearning for the baby. By describing the ordeal the infant faces in a subtle way, you can be sure to arouse oxytocin.

If, on the other hand, you tell a story of a mother walking along a street, without the emotional danger or trauma of ill health and a starving baby, that will not be arousing. It is worth noting that these neurons and hormones are skin deep; you don't have to do much to get them up and running. This hormone also has its downside. Let's reserve that for another post.

4. Dopamine

This is referred to as the reward chemical of the brain. It is secreted when the brain experiences a moment of pleasure, like laughter, or relief from stress. At such moments, there is no threat to survival. It includes moments like having a meal, or enjoying a comedy show. Both the teller and the listener enjoy a dose of dopamine, according to (fMRI) studies.

It is a good deal for both the teller and the listener (audience). This is an essential element for inclusion in the last part of the story arc, ideal for entertaining and relaxing the listener as a payoff for listening. For this to happen, it is important to end the story on a happy, hopeful, or humorous note.

In conclusion, when crafting your stories, ask yourself which hormone you wish to arouse to deepen the impact of your story on your audience. For optimum impact, vary your prose or poetry from sad to happy, from tense to exhilarating, or from cool to shock, and anger to excitement. Such variation will keep the listeners experiencing highs and lows.

Stories That Engage and Elicit Action

Finding and telling the right story is key to effective engagement. Unfortunately, not all stories are effective or engaging enough. Whereas some stories may get our attention and stir our emotions, others are bland, tasteless or disgusting.

So what makes a story engaging?

Dr. Paul J. Zak has conducted laboratory studies that indicate emotionally engaging stories receive more donations for a non-profit organization. The situation is, however, very different when a flat or boring story is told without the core elements of the story act. Two groups of individuals were shown two short videos. One group watched a boy and his father at the zoo. The other group watched an emotionally draining video of a father and his son, who is sick with terminal cancer.

"Blood tests of the study's participants showed elevated levels of cortisol (linked to distress), and oxytocin (linked to empathy), in those who watched the emotional video. The other video did not produce the same response. Dr. Zak's research team concluded that narrative actually has the power to change behavior by changing our brain chemistry."

Dr. Zak points out, "The most active areas for the emotional story were the areas in the brain associated with theory of mind, or having an understanding of what others are doing, or going through. This area is rich in oxytocin receptors that make us feel empathy."

Dr. Zak has referenced the work story arc or **Freytag's Pyramid by Gustave Freytag.**

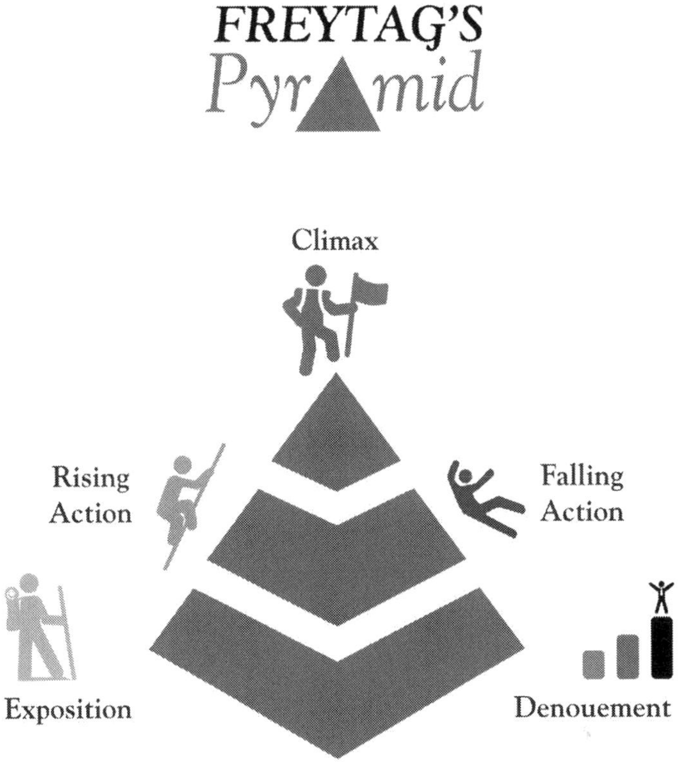

This part of the story provides information about the setting, the backstories, and events occurring before the main plot.

Rising Action

These are a series of related incidents that build up to the point of utmost interest. Without these events, the climax will not stand properly.

Climax

The turning point at which there is a turnaround, from good to evil, or from evil to good.

Falling Action

In this part of the story, the conflict between the protagonist and antagonist unravels, and there is a semblance of victory, one way or the other. It could also have a last phase of suspense.

Denouement

This refers to the resolution, revelation or conclusion. It may capture issues such as release of tension, restoration of peace and new lessons learned.

Not all stories involve rising and falling action, as most storytelling authors teach. There is an alternative.

You can equally have an engaging story in which the protagonist falls into a "Deep Dark Basement" even before experiencing any rise in their fortunes. What makes such a story engaging is not the fall. The fall however, gives the story new energy. It creates uncertainty, empathy and suspense. It also gets the audience's sympathy or emotional involvement by way of rooting or doubting how the protagonist will find his or her way back to safety. Notice that the fall happens in Freedom Land, however if protagonist is able to fight with the demons in the Deep Dark Basement, he or she re-emerges on the other side as a Hero in the Promise Land.

An Alternative Interpretation to an Engaging Story (Death Crawl Concept)

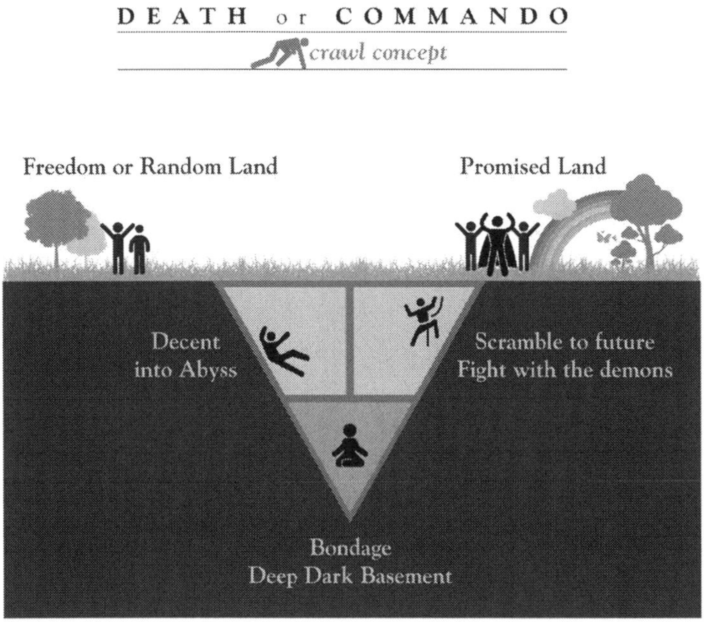

What this Means for Professionals who Often Present to Groups

As a leader, educator, or business owner, it is important that you choose your stories carefully. This can make or break critical moments. Some stories can depress your audience for a long time. Others can uplift and inspire for a long time. Through them, you can penetrate the minds of your audience like a Trojan horse.

In essence, stories and narratives offer a unique opportunity to engage the theory of the mind's capacity to make sense of the world. Use this ability with compelling characters, whose longings and frustrations are similar to those of your audience.

Every Word Counts

All words are not born the same. Some are charged, some are uncouth, and some are vague. Every word you use is born with a mathematical sign: positive (+), negative (-) and neutral (0). Words can actually be mapped on the number line. For a very important conversation, it is important to map out your choice of words carefully. Here is an example to illustrate the power of this? You'd notice that one of the words is certainly weaker than the other. If you want to elicit the best possible (optimum emotional and hormonal) response, try to choose your words very carefully. As a rule of the thumb, try to leave your audience on a more upbeat and hopeful tone.

-10 -9 -8 -7 -6 -5 -4 -3 -2 -1 0 +1 +2 +3 +4 +5 +6 +7 +8 +9 +10

Plot the following pairings of words on the number line:

1. Compliment and Congratulations
2. Brush and Crush
3. Destroy and Dismantle
4. Invent and Develop
5. Cream and Lotion
6. Season and Phase
7. Electrocute and Shock
8. Mermaid and Fairy

9. King and Queen
10. Fantasy and Dream

Hopefully, you noticed that some of the words are more potent than others. This is an indication that when you are crafting your story, close attention to your choice of words can go a long way in insinuating or generating a different picture in the mind of your audience. Take, for example, the words *brush* and *crush*. They are very similar, but one is far stronger. On the negative scale, I will place brush as a -2; however, crush will definitely be a -8 in my mind.

In light of the above, you can see that different words stir a different level of emotion. With respect to words, fMRI (a functional neuroimaging technology that measures brain activity by detecting associated changes in blood flow and how this impacts human actions) studies have shown that there is brain activity in response to words. Words like coffee or perfume elicit activity in the olfactory cortex of the brain. On the contrary, neutral words such as chair or key do not get such neural activity.

Metaphors used in context, such as, "a singer with a baritone voice," or "the director had leathery hands," also lit up the sensory cortex of the brain. On the contrary, "the singer had a pleasing voice," and "the director had strong hands," did not get any neural activity.

Similar neural activities have also been revealed by fMRI scans with respect to motor activities, which are registered in the motor cortex. Descriptions for arm and leg movements have different locations, indicating that the brain is capable of responding to very specific words or phrases, such as, *John grabbed the object*, or *Terry kicked the ball.*

With respect to perception, researchers believe the brain does not make much of a distinction between reading about an experience and encountering it in real life, because in each case, the same neurological regions are stimulated.

This is one aspect of understanding how the brain works that teachers, entrepreneurs and leaders can take advantage of in crafting stimulating stories to persuade their followers about what to do.

Simulate and Stimulate the Brain by Making a Movie in the Mind of Your Audience

Have you ever read a novel that transports you into a very different world, or takes you to a place you have never been? This is what it means to use stories to tap and transport your audience into another world. The key to doing this is fictional crafting. Start by creating a scene or situation.

In such a situation, "plant" a human or animal character and give it human qualities. In order to turn on the movie in the mind of the audience, give that character a goal, and at the same time sabotage that aspiration by mounting a wall that stops him or her from reaching the goal.

The rest of the movie depends on how you choose to heighten the tension between the "seeker" and the "stalker," or "stopper." That is the stuff of which good movies are made. President John F. Kennedy's speeches about putting a man on the moon, and returning him safely, fall within this category of moving with narrative. Do you know the impact of that on science, America and the world? Go figure.

Three Ways to Apply Lessons Learned from this Chapter

1. **Collect Real World Examples and Stories**

   Like the military, medicine, law, and other fields of business, you can apply storytelling to your work. Use scenarios, problems faced by the audience, cases you've handled, or items, graphics, and videos you care deeply about.

2. **Use Fictional Energy**

   Alternatively, you can also use your creative license to do the following: create fictional examples, embellish factual examples, appeal to the senses, and paint pictures in the minds of your listeners.

3. **Use Intriguing Energy**

   Be sure to frame the story to also capture the audience's viewpoint, and inject rhetorical questions that pull in the listener. Embed characters that look like and sound like your audience. Use elements of novelty, intrigue, suspense and surprises to grab and retain the gatekeeper, i.e., the amygdala.

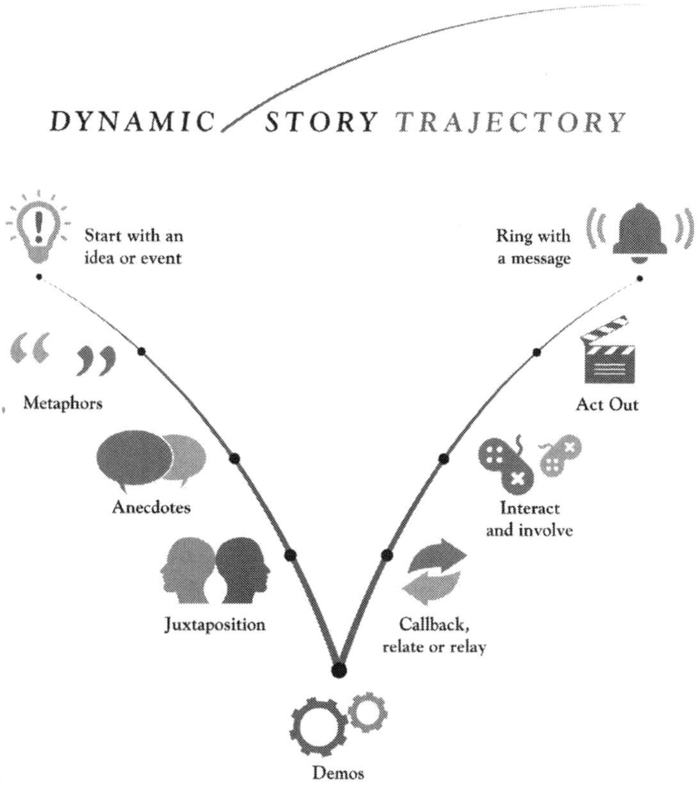
DYNAMIC STORY TRAJECTORY
Start with an idea or event
Ring with a message
Metaphors
Act Out
Anecdotes
Interact and involve
Juxtaposition
Callback, relate or relay
Demos

Chapter 2:

How to Craft Engaging Stories that Win Hearts & Minds in the Boardrooms, Showrooms and Classrooms

Section 1: What Makes an Engaging Story

The Five Gs (5 Gs) of a Compelling Story

Good writing is a serious craft that takes considerable time to develop and fine-tune. A compelling story comes from compelling writing. By crafting, you ensure that every word counts. When this is done right, you capture your audience intellectually and emotionally.

The five Gs outlined below enable you to easily structure your thoughts when crafting a story. Beware that the best way to drive a story forward is through characters and conflict. Without characters, the story will be lifeless.

Good Guy with Worthwhile Goal

As humans, we are naturally sympathetic toward a good guy. We root for good guys to succeed, and for bad guys to fail. We root for the underdog. To make it interesting, give the good guy a worthwhile goal, such as job hunting to feed his family, or paying his mortgage. In your story, you can make your customer the good guy in search of a goal. If you are a teacher, don't make yourself the good guy; let it be your student.

A while back, I went to speak to a group of young men at a prison in Singapore. We asked them, what they planned on doing upon release. One guy said he wanted to work as hard as possible to buy his mother an artificial leg. That was one heck of a unique goal that won our sympathy. We often root for the good guy because of their noble goal(s). I have come to notice that even a bad guy with a noble goal will also get some support. Now, I am not encouraging you to join the Italian mafia or practice African voodoo under the guise of making money to go and help the the poor in Somalia and Yemen. You get the point.

Goliath Antagonizes the Good Guy

After revealing the good goal, don't make it too easy for the good guy. Throw in a couple of bad guys to mount a series of roadblocks to thwart the good guy. These obstacles, or detours, add intensity to the story. They also make it more interesting and intriguing.

Grueling Conflict Ensues

In writing the story, give your protagonist some human flaws. His failures and shortcomings will make him or her more relatable. In other words, you don't need to sanitize your character(s); otherwise, they won't be credible to your audience.

Guru Comes to the Rescue

The essence of a story is to educate, persuade, or entertain. Thus, use your story to teach or transfer important life lessons to others. The guru is the one that delivers new wisdom that helps the protagonist to see a new reality.

Gift

A good story should have a premise. The premise evolves into the body of the story with all its complications, conflicts, and climax, then ending with a resolution. After the resolution, or what Gustav Freytag refers to as "denouement" or finale, the storyteller owes one more critical element of the story to his or her audience—the gift, or payoff. The gift or payoff sums up the moral of the story in a few words. Words that give the essence of the story or why it was worth telling the story.

Ideally, the gift should be short, sharp, sweet, rhythmic and memorable. In other words, it should be similar to what media people call a sound bite. Here are a few examples: "what goes around, comes around," "you can run, but you can't hide," and "what stumbles in Canada, rumbles in America."

Section 2: Four Types of Stories

Types of Stories Worth Telling to Win Hearts and Minds

This chapter examines four types of stories that can be used to generate interest, educate, build trust, entertain, and move an audience. An example of each type of story is given to strengthen your appreciation for what others are doing. There is also a link that allows you to see an example of the story type in action. Each story ends with a couple of bullet points that identify key learning points or takeaways.

Magnetic Stories Build Buzz, Likability and Interest

Generally, magnetic stories are designed to show, "I care, I am cool, in the know—please like me." Magnetic stories aim at building bridges to reach friends, fans, and followers. They whet the appetite of an audience, prospects, or customers. If you have a **backstory** that led to what you do today, that will make a good magnetic story.

Magnetic stories are embedded with desirable, but humbling social attributes (social currency) to endear a brand to its potential audience, or prospects. Such stories may drop clues here and there, about why you or your organization is different.

Here you can throw in facts and figures that matter, such as: *Three years ago when we started, we had nine rejections out of 10. Today, we have three rejections out of 10. It is not that we have become so good; part of the issue is that the market has shifted.* Ideally, magnetic stories are used to build awareness, or to boost likability and generate curiosity about a brand.

Google Reunion Story

Google uses an emotional story to position its flagship product, i.e., the search engine in India. In the story, the search engine giant narrates how two friends (Yusuf and Baldev), separated decades ago during the India and Pakistan conflict, are reunited, thanks to a Google search. The story demonstrates the power of its search engine, its relevance and its ubiquitousness. It is a polite reminder that Google can unite families and friends. Therefore, it is cool and likeable.

Lessons/Action Steps from Google:

1. Cast your target audience as the winner
2. Cast your brand as the enabler or protagonist
3. Cast a social ill of a broken world (war) as the villain (Goliath)

Google Story link: http://tinyurl.com/ofo72um

Magnetic stories attempt to draw a client or an audience nearer by demonstrating empathy. Without empathy, there is no connection. Ideally, these stories are used to build rapport, likability, and goodwill. When there is rapport, you can then extend the conversation to more serious issues. Deeper down the sales funnel, it is recommended that you use mission, mayhem or mastery stories to close the deal. Depending on the situation, you may not even need to use all the stories in your menu.

Mission Stories – Show Empathy and Build Connections

Mission stories ideally portray the client or customer as the hero or legend. This raises his self-esteem, ego, and makes him feel appreciated. By casting your customer as the king, you elevate your status as the kingmaker.

Mission stories are framed to cast the customers as potentially successful. This ensures that when such a story is shared with a potential customer or audience, they see themselves through the lens of the other successful customers. In other words, they buy the narrative that they, too, will soon be as important.

This is fundamentally a human need. In Maslow's needs hierarchy, self-esteem is higher above physiological needs. Thus, by appealing to this need in clients, they feel appreciated, important and this draws them nearer to you.

Zappos's Funeral Flowers Story

Tony Hsieh, CEO of Zappos, tells a story about a client who tried for a long time to buy a pair of shoes, but she could not find the particular brand of shoes she wanted for her husband. She almost gave up, but incidentally found them on Zappos. She ordered them. Unfortunately, before the shoes arrived, her husband died in a car accident. The customer called to request a return of the items.

Though not stated in the company's procedure manuals, the Zappos customer loyalty officer who received the call bought flowers and sent them over to the bereaved lady on behalf of Zappos. When the flowers were delivered, the bereaved lady was very touched by the gesture. It was simply incredible! She shared the story with over 30 friends and family members who were grieving with her. They were amazed! Most of them were not only moved, but became avid customer advocates of Zappos. It is very likely these friends and family members will share the story with others. That is how stories generate a positive buzz and word of mouth. Word of mouth leads to trust and sales. Once in a while, a story makes a leap from a just invisible instrument of social communication to a tool or an invisible sales force. For that to happen, the story must be so poignant, so fresh, and so resonant, that it becomes irresistible.

Because the story is authentic, and grounded in truth, it resonates, or gets legs. The company did not set out to tell this story, but by being attentive, it was able to capture it and share it. If you pay attention, you will discover similar stories within your organisation. The trick is to capture them before they fade away.

When you capture, craft and tell such inherently infectious or contagious stories, you elevate your brand. More important, you give your prospects something to talk about; that is, how they become your unpaid invisible sales force.

Lessons/Action Steps from Zappos

1. Share the frustrations of your customers.
2. Show them you care about them.
3. Humanize your organization.

Zappos Story Link: https://youtu.be/dV7eliclaZA

Turbo Tax - Make Your Clients the Hero

As you can observe from the video link below, Turbo Tax goes all out to impress its customers with the story of "you." It is a heroic tale of various things done by "you," the hero of the narrative. This implies "you" are also heroes by filing your taxes through Turbo Tax. The story does this in a very simple but highly impactful way, with a long list of worthy things their customers do. The list is not glamorous at all, but the storyteller glamorizes it with a touch of a chirpy, warm, and heroic tone. That is what keeps it real and grounded. Things ordinary people do every day—work, spend time with family, travel, cycle—the narrator turns into heroics with an upbeat tone and adoration.

By putting its clients on a pedestal through work and life events, Turbo Tax succeeds, by putting itself on a platform to serve them. It is done very tastefully, edifying the daily grind of life—the struggles, the ups, the downs, the tears and toils of ordinary men, and why they matter.

The story ends with a gentle call to action. It calls the customers to tell their stories, i.e., by filing their taxes, and using Turbo Tax software to answer simple questions like: did you get married, travel to Timbuktu, buy a new house, have a baby, cycle to work, and more.

Lessons/Action Steps from Turbo Tax

1. Make your client's work a source of pride.
2. Narrate the struggles of life to unite people together.
3. End with a call to action.

Intuit Turbo Tax Link: http://tinyurl.com/nvsabe7

Mission stories show your passion to serve. They show how others dramatize the change we want to see in the world. By learning about how others dramatize their own circumstances in a story, you are more informed on how to better select and craft your stories effectively.

To make mission stories more effective, end with a call to action. Alternatively, end with a message that empowers the customer to act, or to ask questions about your service or product. When this happens, you have the opportunity to draw them in to further explain or close the deal.

With respect to the sales funnel, mission stories are ideal for prospects or customers who have had some basic awareness about you, and want to know more. You can do this by helping them to see how others just like them have benefited from your services. They are your best bet after the magnetic stories.

Mayday Stories - Trials & Tribulations

Successful companies use Mayday stories to reveal their trials and tribulations. This increases their trust quotient. Vulnerability is a very powerful force of attraction, enamel, or glue. It is so powerful because it allows everyone to relate through his or her own insecurities. The secret behind the Mayday or mayhem stories is that they reveal our flaws. This humanizes an organization, or the individuals behind it, thereby building trust.

Trust builds buzz, because flaws become social currency in starting conversations. Here's a quick example, "Do you know that Steve Jobs was once fired from Apple, the company he co-founded?" and, "Do you know that Warren Buffet still lives in the same house he bought 1958?" These are ideal conversation starters to debunk myths or to segue. Mayday stories can also be called crucible stories. In essence, such stories capture the low and difficult moments. This makes for a fascinating story, because the audience wants to find out how things worked out, or got resolved.

Autobiographies of great leaders often have accounts of Mayday stories such as like Mandela's Robin Island days, Gandhi's non-violent protests against the British, Churchill's war years, and more. Businesses, like individuals, also face Maydays or struggles to survive. Customers and prospects love Mayday stories because they are relatable and show the human side of a business entity.

Thus, it is not uncommon to read stories about the early and difficult days of Apple, Starbucks, Southwest Airlines, AirAsia and others in newspapers around the word. Such stories demonstrate that businesses care about making a connection with their customers. As Robert McKee puts it, "stories are the currency of human contact." Without this currency, you are doing your company or business a disservice.

Lego's Trials, Toils and Triumphs

Today, Lego is a world-famous toy maker. This global brand has come a long way from very humble beginnings. Founded well over a century ago in Denmark by Ole Kirk Christiansen, the company has withstood many heart-wrenching setbacks on its way to the world's centre stage.

In the early days, Lego withstood a bankruptcy filing by its first major wholesaler. In subsequent years, the company suffered a devastating fire that consumed its factory. Later on, the toymaker faced other major challenges, such as the adoption and adaptation of plastic bricks as well as other technologies. It has been a long and very tortuous journey for Lego.

Today, besides being a toymaker with theme parks worldwide, it is also a conglomerate, with publishing and other areas of business. Behind the successful company everyone sees today, there are many past setbacks and comebacks.

Lessons/Actions Steps from Lego

1. Start with the founder.
2. Craft a journey story.
3. Show the peaks and valleys.

The Lego Story Link: http://tinyurl.com/cr9n9qv

Every business has faced setbacks and seen comebacks. In order to make a good narrative, pick setbacks that have taught you bigger lessons. By focusing on the critical lessons, it is easier to show how your company defied the obstacles (Goliath) to get where it is today.

To make your story more captivating, make sure that it highlights some of the twists and turns, peaks, valleys, struggles, odds, obstacles, fear, and terror involved in surviving the setbacks. By this, I mean the fights, the fight backs, the tense moments.

When this is done right, the stories come alive and become memorable. Such stories get shared, thereby enhancing brand awareness, and potential influence. The key is to focus on specific turning points, not all turning points.

Mastery Stories - the Springboard

Mastery stories deal with how individuals or organizations turn adversity into opportunity. They capture the past, present and the future. Call them serendipity, or springboard stories; such stories illustrate the capacity to take a bad situation and turn it into a good one. With a bit of reflection, every organization can identify one serendipity story that it can use to attract followers to build a better future. Mastery stories borrow from the past, or from specific examples, to paint a better or more plausible future.

Aria Resort and Casino – How a Resort Tripled Sales with Storytelling

Aria Resort in Las Vegas did its homework. Its business storytelling paid off big time. It increased sales by over

301%! What makes this case study remarkable is that 2009 was very bad for businesses in Nevada; in fact the state was in a recession at that time. Getting noticed in Las Vegas is a daunting task. The competition for tourist dollars is cutthroat. Every casino uses all its "magic tricks." What they are capable of doing to get your attention is indescribable, from the good, the bad, to the downright immoral.

In the midst of all that, Aria Resort espoused good old storytelling, especially online. Here are some lessons on how to use storytelling to increase your lead generation, or to build a buzz in the marketplace about your brand.

1. **Start with a Theme:** A theme gives you focus around which to hoist your messages and stories. As a new resort, Aria made a bold claim to fame: "The Center of Vegas has Shifted." That invited a lot of questions. Which center? Why has it changed?
2. **Use a Hook(s):** A hook enables you to draw the reader into your message. Keep it inviting and relevant. They trumpeted the fact that they had a top quality Japanese restaurant, with a head chef who owned the first Japanese restaurant in the US to earn its three-star Michelin rating.
3. **Reveal Unique Facts:** Such facts make for very interesting reading, and also serve as social currency or conversation starters. Here is one of the dozen facts that Aria capitalized on to gain attention and drive sales. They said their restaurant,

"Blossom," was quiet, and had intimate booths. For the noise averse like me, that is a superb catch.

4. **Share Differentiators:** Differentiators help customers see you as different. Every business has differentiators. Unfortunately, not every business communicates them. Aria said, for example, "Our fish is not out of water more than 24 hours before it is on your plate."
5. **Paint Pictures and Create Imagery:** They shot photos that were "cool, fun, and quick." These were shared online, mainly via Facebook and Twitter. Instead of telling only, they also showed the pictures to complement the stories about cool slot machines as wide as TV screens.
6. **Share Mini-Stories:** The mini-stories were about events, incidents and things happening in and around the facility. Fascinating stories were shared on Facebook and Twitter. This earned them 670,000 friends on Facebook, and 134,000 on Twitter. These numbers were an indication of clout.
7. **Tagline & Hashtags:** In social media, both the tagline and hashtags help in the search and classification of information. This allowed them to aggregate, share, curate and re-share with their fans and followers. It also made for easier reference for their customers.
8. **Focus on Awareness, not Bookings:** To be conservative, put the focus of a campaign on creating awareness. Favorable awareness generates buzz,

and buzz inevitably leads to inquiries (leads) and bookings, or sales. When word of mouth takes over, you are golden.

9. **Be Creative - Use Creative Angles:** From the kitchen to the bar, to the showroom, Aria sought to show things differently. By sharing quirky facts about its food preparation practices, such as only cooking fresh fish, they entered, and then penetrated the hearts of healthy eaters.
10. **Share Across the Board:** Aria made it a point as far as possible to share information across various social media platforms, as opposed to traditional advertisement media with its often forbidding cost. This helped them in that some articles with the theme tagline, "#The Center" were shared over four times. That is resonance, which seldom happens in old advertisements.

The campaign shows that storytelling, even on a shoestring budget, can build buzz, generate prospects, and leads based on awareness and curiosity. Finding a theme, tag lines, taking pictures, posting and sharing insightful mini-stories is not all that impossible to do. I believe most of the ideas are doable, even by smaller companies without big budgets, and that is the reason I have shared it.

Whether you run a big enterprise or not, you can attempt some of the story ideas implemented by Aria Resorts in your business. Start by taking smaller steps.

Lessons/Actions Steps from Aria Resorts

1. Start with a theme.
2. Give the story some depth.
3. Focus on awareness, not sales.

Aria Resort and Casino - http://bit.ly/1mwUO4K

Section 3: The 30-Day Challenge – A 30-Day Cheat Sheet on How to Craft Engaging Stories

Does all this sound daunting? Let me help and save you some time. Over the course of 30 days, just take one easy tool, idea, and technique from the information below and dramatically improve your ability to craft compelling stories.

Each day, I'll share with you one easy way of crafting an engaging story that will earn you instant recognition and respect. My goal is simple. I want to take the mystery and misery out of the process of crafting an engaging story. For over 10 years, my stories have earned me awards in Asia and North America, my goofy accent and some daunting circumstances notwithstanding. Stick with me for 30 days, and be willing to craft mini-stories of about 100 words per day. That's all. Once complete, share with your friends, on Facebook, Twitter or Google+.

I've studied this craft obsessively for over 12 years. The last time I checked, I've studied over 83 published authors, excluding hundreds of hours of learning from some of the top coaches in the world. Now, I am just getting warmed up.

I've tried to capture the very best of my Eastern, Western, Northern and Southern exposure and experiences. You're in for a treat. I believe that my cross-cultural exposure has shaped me and my story consciousness profoundly. Below are the finest practical tips I've gathered along the way. You never know how far your story will go. *Four* years after I shared a story in Phoenix, Arizona, someone who was in the audience remembered the story, and me. You want to know the sweetest part? He doubled my hourly allowance for my summer 2009 internship project while in graduate school. He raised my hourly rate from $23 to $43! That's the power of a well-crafted story. It has staying power. Yes. Its value far exceeds your initial investment. This unique asset called storytelling will serve you as:

- An attention-getter in a noisy and crowded marketplace. Attention is currency!
- A seed-planter – it plants ideas into the minds of listeners
- A simulator – stories simulate and stimulate action
- An Emodutainer – emotionally engage, educate and entertain
- A trust-builder – a vehicle for sharing your values and mobilizing.

Day One: Analogy Gets Instant Attention

"A good teacher, like a good entertainer first must hold his audience's attention, then he can teach his lesson." John Henrik Clarke

Start with an attention-grabber such as an **analogy**. Alternatively, start with a bold declaration, or a question that disrupts the status quo. Perhaps you can say, "Mr. Quek is the rock of our company. He is steadfast, solid and seldom sick. Oh boy! For over 20 years, he has been the one man that everyone calls upon when their computer breaks down, or when there is a water leakage, late delivery of pizza for a staff birth day party, a missing memo, an over-booked auditorium or missing box of dark chocolates from the pantry. Mr. Quek is every company's dream team player. Not bad for a guy who is the CEO of small Chinese bakery with 120 staff.

That's a short analogy. Now, tell a story about someone who is the rock of your life. It does not have to be someone that is obvious. The more unusual your analogy, the better. This analogy breaks the ice. It will also:

- Get the audience's attention
- Get them ready to read, or listen to the rest of your story
- Whet their appetite
- Allow you to set the tone right up front
- Get you noticed for the right reasons.

Day Two: Backstory Builds Empathy

"People don't buy what you do; they buy ***why*** *you do it. And what you do simply proves what you believe." Simon Sinek*

A **backstory** is a story that enables the audience to care about you and your aspirations. It shares a picture of the past, vis a vis a character's ambitions and struggles. This gets the audience to start rooting for a character by **making that character likable.**

If you own a business, your backstory is your *igniting incident*, i.e., the issue that motivated you to be in business. What inspired you, and how will this shape your future, and the future of others that depend on you? Backstories:

- build credibility
- show authenticity
- make you unique and special
- earn empathy
- generate advocates

Day Three: Characters in Conflict Galvanize Stories

"Character is a diamond that scratches every other stone." Cyrus A. Bartol

Stories with characters in conflict create tension. This raises the stakes. For a story to be engaging, cast one employee who embodies the values of your company versus a major challenge.

Here's an example: write a story that humanizes your organization, showing a typical day in the life of one employee serving the company during a poor weather situation. This type of galvanizing story:

- puts one face on an organization with thousands
- makes your organization relatable
- makes you real and genuine
- sheds life on your otherwise purely technical areas
- shows your behind-the-scenes commitment

Day Four: Dialogue Drives Story

"She said, 'What?' so I replied, 'what?' She gave me a look that said, 'What, what?' and I didn't respond, because I fell in love with her." Jarod Kintz

Dialogue is the fuel of a story. It keeps the audience second-guessing the next move or word. It draws them in. By so doing, they take sides, and by so doing, become part of the fray. Good dialogue is short, sharp, and organic. It exhibits human flaws, greed, and biases. Craft a story that captures something remarkable that happened to you this week, like a conversation you had with your boss, a colleague, or someone at the water cooler.

- What intriguing thing did he or she say?
- Show two viewpoints
- Show a bit of greed, or a flaw
- Show one vulnerable character

Show how our biases taint our judgment.

Day 5: Emodutainment is the Key to Engagement

"Art is moral passion married to entertainment. Moral passion without entertainment is propaganda, and entertainment without moral passion is television." ~Rita Mae Brown

Some stories are three-dimensional. They are emotionally touching, message-rich, and funny.

When fused in the right proportions, such stories are epic. They are also capable of taking an audience from a deep, dark basement to the top of Everest.

Think of an embarrassing moment you've had. Share it with sincerity; let the audience laugh at your expense. Cut it short to inject a serious question to draw your audience in, and then unleash a new twist. Audiences like tragedy, mixed with sincerity and hilarity. It generates empathy. It helps you to:

- connect deeper
- elicit empathy
- uplift them by depressing yourself
- cheer them with your tragedy
- teach a lasting lesson

Day 6: Facts & Factoids Fascinate

"It is the absence of facts that frightens people: it is the gap you open, into which they pour their fears, fantasies, and desires." Hilary Mantel

Some facts about you are simply interesting. Others are unique or insightful. Do you have a unique hobby, like collecting seashells or toothpicks, old typewriters, antique furniture, sex toys, rock climbing equipment from Nepal or musical flutes from around the world? I know an American friend that collects various brands of wooden African hand-held pianos "mbiras." Use such unique facts to tell a magnetic story that gets you some notoriety.

Alternatively, you can share unique events, ceremonial rites or intriguing aspects of your personal life. Have you ever climbed a forbidden fence or tree? What kind of tree was it? Was an oak tree, a fruit tree or Christmas tree? Turn the facts into compelling story. Such a story is born of social currency.

One of my friends met his wife at the back of an ambulance. Using such a fact or factoid earns you:

- instant curiosity currency
- respect and reverence
- attention
- endearment

Day 7: Gift is the Goal of Story

"May it be a light to you in dark places, when all other lights go out." *J. R. R. Tolkien*

Every story must end with a gift or a message that sums up the purpose of the story. Before sharing a story, ask yourself, what is the message or essence of this story to the audience? When the message is clear, the story is a winner. Share an eye-opening moment you have experienced this year. End with a message that is concise. Keep the message short, so that it is:

- memorable catchy and rhythmic
- upbeat and inspiring "kissable," i.e., keep it short and simple (kiss)
- understandable to a fifth grader.

Day 8: Humanize to Colonize Their Minds

"Acting is nothing more or less than playing. The idea is to humanize life." *George Eliot*

Stories are compelling vehicles to convey information and emotions. The human brain loves tales of imperfections in other people. Such stories make us profoundly human. Don't hide flaws. Show us how a character was caught with his or her hand in the cookie jar.

Share a story about a time that you were caught red-handed. Let the story show your human flaws—perhaps a little indulgence that turned awry. Such stories are about:

- trials and tribulations
- imperfections
- frustrations
- some unexpected trauma you've faced, thanks to your own actions or stupidity.

Day 9: Invoke Insecurities for Alignment

"The problem with human attraction is not knowing if it will be returned." *Becca Fitzpatrick, Hush, Hush*

Everyone has something that they don't want the world to find out. If you want to engage and connect deeper with your audience, acknowledge some of these issues. Do it politely. Don't rub salt against the wound by using it to insult or berate your audience. Uplift, don't depress. Tell a story that expresses one of your insecurities. Such stories can potentially earn you goodwill for:

- sincerity
- trustworthiness
- authenticity
- honesty

Day 10: Jazz it Up for Comic Relief

"When the music changes, so does the dance." *African proverb*

Tell a story that sticks to the facts. Only embellish for comic or poetic relief. You have the creative license to embellish, but please, stick to the facts. If it is fictional, let the audience know. If you fail to do that, you are not helping your reputation. Jazzing up a story helps you to achieve the following elements of dynamic engagement:

- emodutainment
- uncover some genius moments

- transcend physical limitations
- add a touch of fiction or non-fiction turn tragedy into comedy

Day 11: Values That Drive Your Vision

"It's not hard to make decisions when you know what your values are."   Roy Disney

Instead of telling your employees, "Our core value is to 'put the customer before profit,'" tell a story that illustrates how you arrived at this value or principle. When you share a story that underlies those values, your employee(s) remember it longer. Share a story that introduces one of your core principles in life. Craft it carefully. It will help your audience get to know you better. The story makes values more: digestible;

- discernable
- encouraging, but not pushy
- more relatable
- memorable

Day 12: Fables for Touchy-Feely Issues

"My journey in life, my footprints in the world."   Laila Gifta Akita

Fables are succinct stories, often involving animal characters. Do you recall the story of the tortoise and the hare? Why not make up your own story about the hippo and the cheetah? The key is to personify one animal of your choice (give it human qualities). The animal could represent the government, enemy, or even your mother-in-law. With animal characters, address:

- controversies
- counter-culture ideas
- revolutions
- sensitive topics
- thought-provoking questions
- gossip

Day 13: Magic Moments Make an Unforgettable Story

"My life is my message." Mahatma Ghandi

Magic moments are uniquely captivating moments that ring strong in the mind of the audience. They are memorable and long lasting, even several hours, days, or years after listening to a story. The more of such moments you have in your story, the better. A story with magic moments is unforgettable. Tell a story about the best speaker or speech you've listened to in the last few years. What exact moment in the speech or story do you still remember? What did the speaker express? You can start with, "I will never forget the day I listened to my commencement speaker say, "if the youths of today are bad, it is because our society is worse." Let your story capture such unforgettable moments

- sound bites (finely-coined phrases)
- moments of deep connection
- compelling picture

- dripping emotion
- a moment of rare courage

Day 14: Narrate to Calibrate the Tempo

"In a thriller, the camera's an active narrator, or can be." *John McTiernan*

For a story to be compelling, it must move back and forth between narration and dialogue. In essence, the narration calibrates the scene for conflict, or collision of forces. Without narration, the audience will be too caught up in the tensions, and they may suffer conflict fatigue. Retell an incident from your professional life, in which an underdog taught you an important lesson. Start by narrating what happened, just before you enter the scene in which the underdog taught you something unforgettable. You can start with, "Long before I got to know Ben, I always thought he was an absolute loser ..." Let your narration do the following:

- set the scene
- build up some tension
- tell the backstories of key characters
- serve as an antidote to a highly emotional climax
- foreshadow

Day 15: Onomatopoeia

"If you want to succeed, you should strike out on new paths, rather than travel the worn paths of accepted success." *John D. Rockefeller*

In telling your story, use sounds that resemble what you are describing. These will enhance the audience's auditory appreciation and connection to the story. The use of onomatopoeia deepens a story's connection to reality, e.g., a dog growls while a cat meows. We all know that some sounds define a place. Both a church and a mosque are religious places, but they have different, unique sounds. Use onomatopoeia to describe a day you spent at the dentist, or at church. Add sounds to scare or endear us to your place of choice. This will:

- show the uniqueness of place
- add sounds to convey what goes on, like ambulance siren, or papers rustling
- create a feel of the place just with sound

Day 16: Paint Pictures with Words

"It's the little details that are vital. Little things make big things happen." *John Wooden*

Details matter. Water is made of molecules. Pictures are made of pixels. Without pixels, you can't have masterpiece portraits. Sorry, not even your selfies.

Details are the building blocks of mastery. When your story has vivid details, it speaks. Just enough details. Not too much, and not too little. It's like salt in food. Share a story about an item that you love very much. It could be your piano, a parachute, a flute, a paintbrush, or in my case, the harmonica. Paint a picture of why this item is special to you. You can start with, "When I play my harmonica in my room alone, I feel like a rock star in front of a thousand screaming fans. I can sec their bright faces, their smiles; I can feel their echoes. Oh, I love it …" Tell a short story about your love affair with a special item in your life. Make an effort to:

- be as visual as possible
- paint pictures with tiny details: shape, size, color, texture, weight
- capture the imagination with sensory details
- make it visible in the mind's eye

Day 17: Questions that Sustain Engagement

"Status quos are made to be broken." *Ray Davis*

Use questions as hooks to draw your audience into the conflict, or the issues at stake. By asking a question about an issue that is relevant, you get your audience to stop thinking about other things, and focus on what you present. Ask a rhetorical or even a silly question, and see what happens. Suddenly, everyone looks up. Ideally, use your questions to direct your conversation or storytelling. Tell a short story about a bad day at the office. Start by asking, "Have you ever had a bad day at the office?" Then launch forward to tell your story, capturing the following:

- what happened
- who the bad boy or situation was
- who helped you out
- the implications of the issue on work life today
- what you learned from the story.

Day 18: Resolve any Raging Issues

"You can't put a limit on anything. The more you dream, the farther you get." *Michael Phelps*

In a story, you owe it to your audience to resolve any tensions or conflict you have generated. Resolution gives closure. Without closure, there is suspense and uncertainty. In other words, let your audience know what the outcome of the brawl was, or the indictment, the grand jury, or whatever issue was at stake. This enables them to:

- agree or disagree with you
- make up their own minds on the ethics of the issue
- know what to expect the next time they encounter a similar situation
- have a better understanding of other points of view
- learn something about another context
- develop a new perspective

Day 19: Suspense Stirs Deeper Emotions

"Suspense is worse than disappointment." *Robert Burns*

Suspense is the stuff of which good stories are made. It gets the audience to lean forward. One way to create suspense is to dangle something precious, but don't give it away—not just yet. Delay it until maturity. That keeps the audience awake, and guessing the outcome.

Tell a story with a big mystery from the very start. Slowly release clues, but don't release all. Build up the energy and suspense until the right moment. The first clue sets up the second. The second sets up the third, and so on. Use this technique to build suspense in your story. Make a point of:

- making a big promise, e.g., "My grandfather died at 50—it was an unnatural death"
- asking a question that stimulates more curiosity, e.g., have you ever lost someone in his prime?
- slowly give some clues leading up to the big, unnatural death
- only giving away the big revelation at the end.

Day 20: Trip Up the Protagonist to Create Panic

"It's as boring to see a completely evil villain as it is to see a completely good guy." *Brian Helgeland*

People often root for the good guy. I mean a good guy with a good goal or purpose. Audiences like to root for good guys with a worthwhile purpose. It is human nature, however it is not good enough to sustain interest over a longer period of time. In other words, to sustain their interest, there must be some twists, turns and complications.

Once the good guy has been established, put him through a few good rounds of success, and then suddenly turn the odds against him. Put him in an awful situation. It could be something such as a wrongful arrest or detention for crime he did not commit. That will terrify your audience, or whoever was rooting for him. At the same time, it deepens their level of engagement. This complication will make your story more interesting because:

- it engenders creative anxiety
- it suddenly generates new energy
- a new twist creates uneasy emotions
- it gets the audience to be more emotionally involved
- it ties the audience into anticipating the outcome
- it is a test of character

Day 21: Use Utopia to Create Euphoria

"We learn the rope of life by untying its knots." Jean Tommer

You can use a fictional story of an illusory place (utopia) to address any "elephants in the room," or hot-button issues that nobody wants to talk about. The best way to start such a story is by saying, "Imagine a world in which …" Once you've obtained that creative license, you can then create your fictional or utopian world, with any characters, names, or places of your imagination. Share a fictional story about a city only you know about. Use it as a metaphor for what happens in your organization, e.g., the mayor is the CEO. Be sure to:

- make it non-invasive
- keep it light, and easy to understand or compare
- be subtle and polite in asserting your points of view
- use the impersonal "third person, singular" voice

- end with a key lesson that is applicable to your organization

Day 22: Verisimilitude Shows Authenticity

"Merely corroborative detail, intended to give artistic verisimilitude to an otherwise bald and unconvincing narrative." *W. S. Gilbert*

Verisimilitude gives the reader a sense of place: the look, feel, sound, or whatever defines a place. Is it a home, an office or a space shuttle? Let the description depict it vividly, to show tiny details, such as cigarette butts, labels on the wall, the smell of vodka, half-empty bottles, music from the roof, entertainers, etc. Tell a story that depicts a unique place from your childhood. What does it remind you of:

- nostalgia
- simplicity
- ambition
- remorse
- anger
- futility
- hopelessness

Day 23: Weave in Drama and Karma

"Habit is a cable; we weave a thread of it each day, and at last, we cannot break it." *Horace Mann*

You cannot afford to be boring. You owe it to your audience to infuse your stories with drama and karma. By drawing from both ends of the spectrum, they keep the story pregnant with meaning. Share a story about your rise and fall during your early career. Infuse your story with the following:

- new discoveries
- twists and turns
- shocks and upsets
- trips and turns
- stumbles and fumbles

Day 24: X-ray Society's Sick Ways

A storyteller uses his wit and wisdom to x-ray the problems and issues that people face, and yet don't have the courage to speak up about. If a storyteller fails to project existing issues that plague people, then he or she has failed in the salient mission of being a gatekeeper. To earn your relevance, tell stories that matter, stories that uplift, but don't depress people. Tell stories that touch on the issues on their minds that they are wrestling with, as in Animal Farm or in the movie Avatar. Share a story in which you take a very forceful stand against an issue facing your profession. Use the voice of an advocate to x-ray:

- invisible undercurrents
- the silent majority
- a vocal minority
- anything that will affect the next generation
- a point of view
- an obsolete law
- the middle of the road

Day 25: Yodarize with Euphemisms

"Do or do not. There is no try." *Yoda*

This means you should give a very distinct voice and meaning to an issue. Do that via a very unique or queer character, like Yoda. Walt Disney has Mickey Mouse. Star Wars has Yoda.

Create a compelling character that attacks one social issue in your field. Use this character to tell a story about the challenges and aspirations of a neglected minority in your field. Let your unique character offer some wisdom about:

- a desired course of action
- the outcome of silence
- how ignorance is so poisonous
- why peace is not guaranteed
- action is key

Day 26: Zero in on the Ambience

"The best measure of a man's honesty isn't his income tax return. It's the zero adjust on his bathroom scale." Arthur C. Clarke

By zeroing in, you give the reader or the audience a front row seat. It is up-close to the drama that is unfolding onstage. It opens up a fresh window of sight into a story's ambience and intricacies.

Craig Valentine's 1999 World Champion of Public Speaking teaches a VAKS approach to zeroing in. VAKS stands for the "visual, auditory, kinesthetic, and smells" of a place. When those elements come together, the reader gets a feel of the ambience.

Share a story about your favorite pet, and how you connected with it. You can start with, “If you’d been a fly on the wall of my balcony Sunday morning, you’d have seen me playing with my German shepherd at ...” Using VAKS, zero in to show your audience the:

- colors
- textures
- smells
- noises
- whispers
- feel

Day 27: Juxtapose the Good and Gruesome

“Creativity is that marvelous capacity to grasp mutually distinct realities, and draw a spark from their juxtaposition.” Marx Ernst

One way to make your story interesting is to compare very unrelated concepts. This draws into focus two divergent ideas. For example, you can compare politicians to jellyfish. Both are slippery and colorful. You can also juxtapose entrepreneurs with orchestra directors. Both have to make things happen. Tell a story in which you start out by comparing two distinctly unrelated concepts or issues. Help your audience to see how both are:

- related
- similar but different

- fictionally real, but not literally real
- sometimes subject to unfair conclusions
- not exactly the same
- subject to flawed comparisons

Day 28: Metaphorize for Meaning

"Metaphors have a way of holding the most truth in the least space." Orson Scott Card, Alvin Journeyman

A metaphor is a figure of speech that asserts that something is the same as another known object. It can transform the understanding of an issue by demystifying complexity. Years ago, I once told my mother in Africa that the Internet is an invisible information superhighway with no cars. It saved my day!

In a way, a metaphor breathes new life and soul into a complicated issue or subject. Tell a story with a metaphor about a business leader. Show how being a leader can:

- make a difference
- create new ideas
- improve lives
- solve problems
- create more problems

Day 29: Anaphorize to Make it Stick

"She stands, she sits, she staggers, she falls, she dies." Frederick Douglass

Anaphora is a rhetorical device that repeats a word, phrase, or sentence to emphasise meaning, message, urgency, or some critical element of your story. It is partly what made Martin Luther King's "I have a dream," speech very famous. That adds to the other qualities, like the prophetic and poetic elements. Share your signature story with a few words or phrases that emphasize the crux of your message, such as:

- urgency
- rhythm
- clarity
- importance
- increased shelf life

Day 30: Callback Shows Brilliance

"That is, we're into a whole new world with the Internet, and whenever we sort of cross another plateau in our development ... So this is a replay of things that have happened throughout our history." *Bill Clinton*

Callback is a reference to a previously shared idea, joke, storyline, statement, or anything that the audience or listener had grasped from earlier on. It is a very effective technique of reminding or connecting the past to the present in a very intelligent way. Comedians use this technique often to connect ideas, and also to connect deeper with their audience.

As a storyteller, reference a line, statistic, or key phrase in your opening, and subsequently at the end, or in thc conclusion. That will suggest to the audience one or more of the following:

- connecting related ideas
- signaling a similarity
- a reminder of importance
- symbolizing closure

You never know whom your story will touch, encourage, or inspire to change his or her life for the better. Keep telling your story, one person at a time! One concluding thought—Harold Goddard once said, "The destiny of the world is determined less by the battles that are lost and won than by the stories it loves and believes in."

Three Ways to Apply Lessons Learned from This Chapter

1. **Your Story is Your Asset**

   Tell a story about a difficult lesson you've learned in life.

2. **Story for Emodutainment**

   Identify an embarrassing moment you've had in life. Craft a story about the lesson learned.

3. **Types of Stories**

   Find three storytellers you admire. What do you like about them?

Chapter 3:

Closing the Empathy Gap Between the Teller and the Listener

Section 1: How to Close the Empathy Gap to Win Hearts and Minds

Have you ever wondered which story to tell your audience? Tell stories that address the burning or dire needs of your audience. That's the shorter version of the answer. Here is the longer version below.

I'd say your choice of story depends on whether you are speaking to the Eskimos of Greenland or the Bushmen of the Kalahari Desert. Do you want to be known as the guy who sold snow to the Eskimos? That's like selling a mongongo nut to the Bushmen in the Kalahari Desert. Ha-ha-ha. They don't need that. You get the point?

The Story DNA Method

Corporate trainers often do what is called a "Training Needs Analysis." As a leader, teacher or businessperson, you need to do some kind of Reflective Needs Analysis (RNA) to figure out what the audience would be receptive to. By reflecting, you are trying to put yourself in their shoes.

What do they want or need? What are their fears or concerns? What are their aspirations or yearnings, and what are their challenges or obstacles? By attempting to figure out these answers, you are effectively doing what I call a DNA analysis. When you use this *Story DNA Method*, you would connect deeper. You'd earn more respect and admiration. So what does it stand for?

Distressing Matters:

This is something you identify that is causing distress to the audience. By coining a message that reflects their pain, it shows understanding and empathy. It tells them that you care. The audience feels you know their pains, and therefore you are a worthwhile comrade. Often the distresses are tied to something the audience wants to attain.

Ask yourself this question: what is it that they want to have in their lives in the short- to long-term? What will make them happy and fulfilled? Human beings are often motivated by their fears, such as avoidance of the pain of going homeless, loss of income, and loss of face. In other words, they want financial freedom, comfort, social acceptance, and recognition. By addressing the specifics of such results, you give them permission to have the understanding that you care about them.

If you are speaking to a PTA group, you can share the story of a PTA group in another country or region. By highlighting how one parent pursued and obtained special funding for a teen afterschool program that gave parents peace of mind, and kept kids safe, you will hook them. You can add a little statistic, like it reduced teen-related crime by 45%.

Needs:

Regarding the PTA example, needs are things of a practical nature such as books, a lunchtime meal, healthy eating, uniforms, and accessories. By telling a story that addresses these needs directly or indirectly, you tap into an area that parents have to deal with regularly.

If you can figure out what inspires them to start an afterschool garden that produces organic food to supplement the students' kitchen, you are on to something that will get their attention. If, on the other hand, you choose to talk about the excesses of Vladimir Putin's political agenda in Mongolia, because you read a recent book on that topic, you can be sure you will find some parents and even the teacher yawning and looking out the window.

Aspirations:

Another area where you can get their interest is to tell a story that captures the future. What grabs parents and teachers about their children or students? Aspirations such as career ambitions, citizenship, internships, and study abroad programs come right out of the playbook of what parents and teachers are concerned about. Instead of telling a traditional story, you can show a video or share an infographic about a recent study. You can then use that infographic picture as the basis for making a forecast about what will potentially happen when the students graduate in two years.

That will get their attention, because it is on their minds, not your good looks. Sorry. They could care less about your looks, accent, or charisma, but they *would* care about the substance of your talk. Thus, this absolves or vindicates you of any self-doubt with respect to your story itself, because their aspirations take precedence.

If it is possible, end your story with an aspirational message. That will be more enduring and empowering to them, because it will elicit secretions of dopamine, endorphins, and perhaps oxytocin, the rewards and feel-good chemicals of the brain. This will help them remember you for a long time. Such is the power of selecting the right story and message to set their brains on fire.

In essence, the Story DNA Method attempts to marry the underlying science of story with the art. This "holy matrimony" is one that must not be put asunder by anyone. You can put this marriage asunder at your own risk. If you fail to elicit or address some emotions, it could be costly to your connection.

Here is what you need to know: you can't ignore the fears and concerns of your audience and expect to earn their vote of confidence. Is that possible? As social animals, we like to know others care about our needs. For that reason, our dreams, fears and aspirations are a big part of our human condition. These emotions inform, inspire and impact our lives everyday.

In the course of crafting a compelling story, it is important to look into the both the body chemistry, i.e., which neurons or hormones are aroused through the use of words. Your selection of a story or a song has to lend itself to the hormones and emotions you want to ignite or suppress. Ideally this science goes with the art. One guiding post to determine where the distressing issues, needs and aspirations is Maslow's Needs Hierarchy. If you can identify their fears and concerns, you can choose a story that provides hope. Hopefulness ideally comes from dopamine, i.e., the reward chemical of the brain.

Alternatively, if your goal is to instill fear and terror, you need to find a story that will cause them to feel imminent danger, thereby activating the secretion of cortisol. The choice of story for lower level staff such as those in customer service is different from the choice of story for those in the C-Suit. This is so because their fears and aspirations are so different. The military uses some elements of this. On the other hand, if you are speaking to CEOs, your story choice should reflect their aspirations on Maslow's hierarchy.

By using the Maslow's hierarchy as a guide, you'd notice that those are the lower levels of the hierarchy are generally pre-occupied with physiological needs, social needs. On the other hand, those in higher up the hierarchy, tend to prefer esteem and self-actualization needs. A wrong story choice could result in getting the wrong impact emotionally and hormonally. Assume both senior management and lower level staff are on a protest and you had to address them separately; this requires that you choose a different story for each group to frame your talk. For the lower level staff, your story should attempt to close the empathy gap with respect to physiological, safety and belonging needs. On the other hand, for the senior level staff, your story must also be able to frame and discuss issues such as safety, esteem and self-actualization needs.

In summary, story choice must be based on careful and thoughtful reflection. The selection by can have a major impact on the outcome of your presentation. More important, it means the difference between ending with jeers or cheers. **The Story DNA Method** takes guesswork out of this process. Take it seriously.

This matrix below enables you to visually consider and combine the art and science of storytelling with respect to the neuro-science elements outlined in Chapter 1.

Story DNA

DESIRE	NOBEL FIGHT	ATTAINMENT
Distress	Need	Aspiration
Cortisol	Oxytocin	Noble Fight
Anxiety	Uncertainty	Excitement

The core principle of the Story DNA Method is to close the empathy gap between the teller and the audience. You want the audience to feel that you have their best interest at heart. To do that, imagine what the audience thinks, feels and sees capture that in your story. An ideal story therefore combines elements of the matrix above and the illustration below.

EMPATHY / GAP

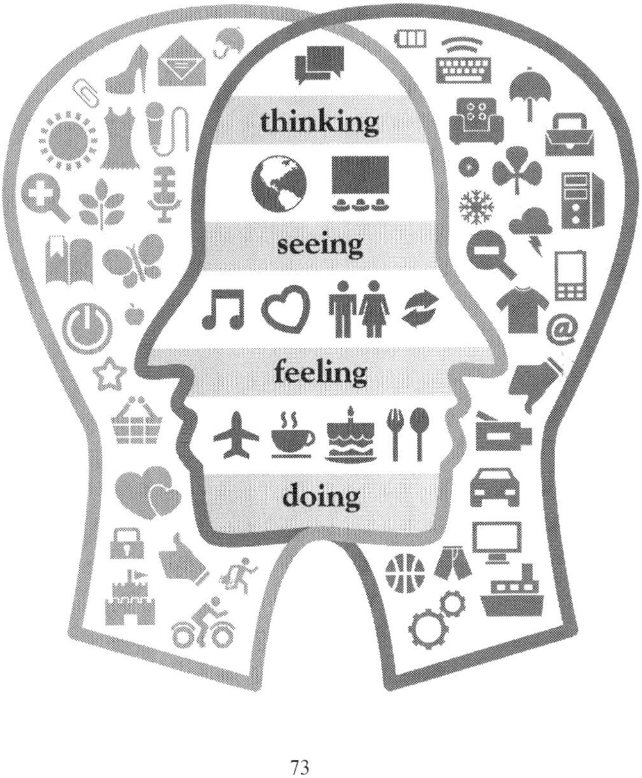

Special Bonus from Gideon

Now that you have your copy of **The Science of Story Selling**, you are on your way to telling breathtaking stories! Remember this; your stories are like an invisible musical instrument that you can use to win the hearts and minds of your prospects for profit or a purpose.

You'll also receive a **special bonus** I've created for you. Add it to your bag of tools. It is what I call *Hollywood Storytelling Secrets for Business Presenters*. It is a study of the key lessons that iconic Hollywood story masters teach their clients. Hopefully, their ideas will inspire you to tell remarkable and memorable stories.

Do you want your stories to be indelible in the minds of your audiences? Start right here.

While *Hollywood Storytelling Secrets* is offered for sale, as a special bonus you can claim it for **free** here:

http://scienceofstorysellingforprofit.com/bookbonus/

The sooner you master these secrets, the better your chances for gaining more likeability and credibility that potentially leads to more profitability.

Let me know if I can be of further help.

Remember: When there is no connection, there is no persuasion,

Gideon F. For-mukwai

Section 2: How to Deepen the Connection with the "Hero's Journey"

The work of American mythologist Joseph Campbell has become widely acknowledged and influential in the making of epic movies. Campbell studied myths from across cultures, and published a book titled, "The Hero with a Thousand Faces." Unlike other scholars of his era that studied differences, he studied similarities.

If you want to connect very deeply with your audience, you can use ideas from Campbell's book by depicting yourself or your organisation in the ordinary world.

1. **Start from the ordinary world.** This allows your audience to see you as one of theirs. Caution—if you start out as a hero, successful and enviable, it is far from relatable. You can't afford to do this, because the audience will see as "special," extraordinary and therefore not relatable.
2. **Call to adventure.** This is a moment when something happens, and you are torn between two worlds: the good and the evil.
3. **Refusal of call to adventure**. Ordinary humans don't jump at every opportunity to fight. Like everyone else, they are afraid, concerned, or torn. Think of the story of Moses in the Bible who was hesitant to lead the Israelites out of bondage in Egypt. He refused to take the call on grounds that he was "slow of speech and tongue." Some commentators believe that Moses may have had a speech impediment.

4. **Meeting with the mentor.** The mentor is the one that challenges the hero, i.e., you, your organization, or volunteers, to undertake the journey with the help of some special tool or knowledge.
5. **Crossing the threshold.** In a story, this is the moment the hero decides that he or she is willing to fight a certain cause, or take arms against a sea of trouble, to use Shakespeare's words. It is a crossing from daylight into darkness or from the ordinary to the scary.
6. **Tests, allies and enemies.** Beyond the crossing, the hero meets with some challenges, and discovers he or she has more enemies, or perhaps has a new friend.
7. **Approach.** Here the hero tries some strategies and wins. He or she realizes that he/she is stronger than once thought. This is a morale and confidence booster.
8. **Ordeal.** This occurs somewhere in the middle of the story. It's a life and death struggle inside of the special world.
9. **Reward.** Often the hero survives the ordeal, or may emerge bruised. Either way, he or she obtains something special that must be brought back. It may be a treasure, or some possession that could be lost again.
10. **Road Back.** The hero's quest is not over after the ordeal. He or she needs to come full circle, i.e., bring back to the ordinary world what was learned from the extraordinary (deep down in

the dark basement - uncertainty, it is gloomy, and dangerous).

11. **Resurrection.** Before the journey can end, the hero must face one last test from the foe, using all he has learned, with everything at stake. This creates deeper suspense and engagement, because everything gained stands at risk on a thin line.
12. **Elixir.** The hero finally makes his or her way back home with the special knowledge that allows him or her to resume life at a higher level.

If you embed elements of this model in your presentation, speeches, and stories, you'll be head and shoulders above the rest. By this, I mean you start by showing how you got involved in what you are currently doing. For example, what were your initial hesitations? Under what circumstances, and why did you take the call to adventure? Who helped you initially as a mentor, and subsequently?

Did you make any friends or foes along the way? What were your early victories that encouraged you? How did that lead you into the darkest days of the ordeal? Assuming you got through the ordeal, what reward or lessons did you learn? Beyond that ordeal, have you had other tough days that tested your faith and strength? How did you overcome them, and what is your biggest secret for the rest of your people?

If you plot this out on a graph—the energy level that enables you to tug the hearts and minds of the audience—you'd notice that using Hero's Journey conveys rises and falls. This ensures that the audience is not bored.

HERO'S journey

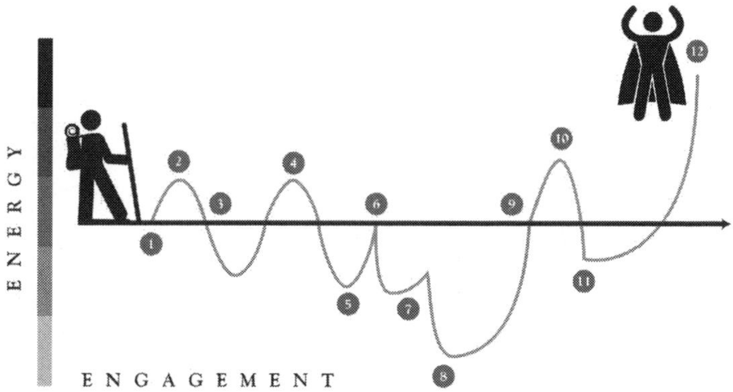

1. Ordinary World - Neutral
2. Call to Adventure - Positive
3. Refusal - Negative
4. Meeting of Mentor - Positive
5. Crossing the Threshold - Positive
6. Test, Friend or Allies - Positive or Negative, depending
7. Approach - Negative
8. Ordeal - Negative
9. Reward - Positive
10. Return - Positive
11. Resurrection - Negative
12. Elixir - Positive

Other Approaches to Creating a Deeper Connection

1. The Ubuntu Approach

If you want to connect deeper with your audience, consider doing as you'd expect others to do to you. There is an old African philosophy that goes, "Umuntu Ngumuntu Ngabantu: "A person is a person because of people." This means that by the way you talk, the way you conduct yourself respectfully, your body, words, and mannerisms convey your humility to those you speak to, be it a small or large group. Have you seen virtuosos bow before an audience? Even rock stars bow. Come to think about it, if such highly talented people do that across all cultures, it speaks to the power of our common humanity, and the importance of humility, not hubris, arrogance and pride. Below, are different ways to connect deeper to, and build rapport with, your audience.

2. Acknowledge the Audience and any Big Egos

You can do this by smiling and nodding as you make your way to the stage or pointing to the person waving "hi" at you. Bill Clinton is exceptionally good at this. His ability to connect with his audience with the subtle body language of acknowledgement is an outlier. Perhaps you can mention the name of some members of the group or audience as you start speaking. Mention the name of some of the behind-the-scenes heroes, not necessarily the powerful names. It tells the audience you do care.

3. Stroke their Egos

Tell them they are a great audience, if they are. It strokes their collective ego. It also shows respect and admiration. You'd be running yourself into the gully if you inform them that you had a better audience the previous day in Beijing.

By acknowledging, complimenting, or stroking their egos, it helps the audience to realize that you do not think too highly of your privilege on the platform, to the point of being dismissive about them. With a deeper connection comes a deeper level of communication. If you want them to see your genius, weave acknowledgment or praise into your story.

4. Connect with a Backstory that Humanizes and Humorizes

Everyone has a backstory. Your backstory could be good, bad, or ugly. Whatever your backstory is, don't let it hold you back. Unfortunately, most of us don't even know that we have self-limiting backstories.

Just because someone made a derogatory comment about your performance, it does not mean that you cannot undo that verbal diatribe. "You cannot let someone's opinion of you become your reality." This quote from Les Brown sums up the importance of looking past your backstory.

Without overcoming your backstory, your future opportunities can be destabilized or damaged. Instead of using those shortcomings as self-limitations, challenge yourself to use those setbacks as stepping-stones to propel you to a greater future.

In 2008, I was asked by a gifted education program director to explain storytelling and presentation skills to some of the smartest high school students in northern Nevada. She then warned me that many of them hated public speaking.

Against that backdrop, I had to plan my opening remarks to alleviate their fears, and reassure them that I was once just like them. I hated public speaking, and I was once the least appreciated kid who spoke at the church in my village.

- *When the other kids spoke at church, all the parents lined up to reward them with money and presents. When I spoke, most parents hid their wallets away, while others instructed the Sunday school teacher to stop putting me in the lineup. At times, only my mom and godmother rewarded me for attempting such speaking. It was a very lonely feeling, I told the students. Some of them had a good laugh at my expense.*

During the course of the talk, I infused my points with stories about how I made some changes, and many mentors helped me along the way. Thanks to their help and the effort I made, I was the champion speaker at the institution where they were attending the training, University of Nevada, Reno, that year. Thus, I encouraged them that with some effort, they too could go on to overcome their fear of public speaking because:

- Sometimes in life you win, just by trying or showing up.

- With effort, we can go from humiliation to getting traction.
- Everyone has some fear; those who win walk through their fear or "feel the fear and do it anyway".
- Even though I graduated nearly at the bottom of my class, I went on to be hired by a major multinational corporation. A few months after starting, I coached a few top students from my former faculty to get jobs at the same corporation where I was then serving as one of two deputy directors.

In my conclusion, I told them that if we aspire to do better in life, we must deliberately find ways to regularly remind ourselves that today's challenges are different from yesterday's obstacles. In order to have a better tomorrow, we must never let our backstory sabotage our future story.

From a very tepid and uncertain start, I ended up having very inspiring participation from the teenagers. They were some of the best I've ever worked with. I was retained for three sequential years to train subsequent groups of students until I left Nevada in 2011.

5. Connect by Using the Titanium Rule

The Golden Rule says, "**Do unto others as you would have them do unto you.**" In a multi-cultural world, the Golden Rule is not enough. It sounds very wholesome, but George Bernard Shaw, in his infinite wisdom, cautions us, "Do not do unto others as you would they do unto you, because their taste may not be the same." Shaw has a point. The Golden Rule assumes that we are all the same. We are similar, but we are not the same, culturally. Connecting deeper in a Western setting is obviously different from an Eastern setting.

We tend to have different cultural references, norms and expectations. Even as individuals, we do. This is where the Titanium Rule comes to your rescue. Claire Raines refers to the Titanium Rule as, **"Do unto others according to their druthers."** If you want to connect deeper with people of different backgrounds, be willing to **"tune into the other individual's preferences."** Even at individual level, we have unique preferences.

To connect deeper with an individual, learn about their **"druthers."** Are they straightforward or diplomatic? Boisterous or withdrawn? Casual or formal? Scattered or focused? Spontaneous or reserved? What is their style of dress—mellow or flamboyant? What are their mannerisms at work—a cluttered desk or spotless workspace? Their speech pattern? Is it hesitant, measured?

6. Connect with Sincerity and Vulnerability

Last summer, I was invited to speak at a major conference in the Sultanate of Brunei Darussalam, South East Asia. It was my first time there. Naturally, I was both excited and a little bit nervous. Prior to the trip, I did some research about the culture, the people, the history, and a host of other issues relating to safety. To help me prepare for my presentation in Brunei, I went to a friend from Brunei who was living in Singapore at the time, to get a few basic phrases in the local language. He was very kind. The few minutes I spent learning the phrases paid off very well.

When I arrived, I started by saying "Asalai mai lekum." To my utmost satisfaction, they replied in unison, "Malaikum Salla." It was just awesome, and for two to three seconds, I was on cloud nine. I said a few more words, and then indicated I would continue in English. As I made the switchover, I saw positive expressions of endorsement on their faces. They came away very satisfied, and were very receptive of my effort, notwithstanding the fact that I probably did not sound like anything close to a native speaker. The icing on the cake is that I earned the accolade of being the second best speaker from the whole conference with over 25 speakers. The big lesson for me was that, with a little effort, you could go a long in deepening your connection with the audience.

7. Connect By Knowing Who You Are - Are You a Samaritan, Scientist or Soldier?

Who are you? What's your mission on earth? Are you a Samaritan, a scientist or a soldier?

Samaritans come to heal a broken world. Scientists come to find missing pieces. Soldiers come to fight and protect. You can only be one at a time. Each one has a special duty or role.

Your role determines your story plot, and your plot determines your mission.

Your mission determines your journey. Your journey determines your story. Your story determines how far you go in life. But you can't determine how far your story will go.

Beware of Barriers to a Deeper Audience Connection

When it comes to connecting deeply with your followers, there are three barriers to connecting with them that entrepreneurs and leaders are often guilty of. When you give your audience the impression that you are superior or special, this disconnects, even if they don't tell you. They stop rooting for you! By understanding these three barriers, you can build stronger bridges of connection. This will enable you to build rapport without undermining your prestige or status as the leader of the team. This gives you greater legitimacy and bandwidth to influence when the need arises.

Barrier #1: Full of Airs

Don't be a prima donna! Don't live in a bubble and expect to connect deeply with your audience. Keep it simple. We are all mortals, and you are not any different. When you have no airs about you, they'll forgive you when you err.

Barrier #2: Show Vulnerability

Everyone has some flaws. Don't pretend to be perfect, because you are not. When you try to conceal your shortcomings, you are implying that they conceal theirs. That's not good for business! When you let them know you are genuine and have some flaws, you earn their deeper trust.

Barrier #3: Avoid the Bandwagon

The next time you see a big wagon passing by, don't just jump on it, unless you have had a sense of where it will lead you and your audience. Does it allow you to reach your goals with them? Think before you leap, because once on board, disembarking is tricky while your team is watching you.

By acknowledging a time you were wrong and showing sincerity, you will be able to connect deeper with your audience. This will open the floodgates of connection and communication for you.

Section 3: Preparing for a Deliberative Delivery

Power of Preparation

Preparation gives you an edge over those who are not as prepared. It means you've had the benefit of thinking things through, which includes the good, the bad, and the ugly. In practical terms, it means you've explored the odds, the opportunities, and the options you have to reach the heart of your audience. Without preparation, you have no edge or vantage point over your adversaries. Talent is not enough. Talent must be combined with concerted orchestration and preparation to yield outstanding results. Some call it nurture. I call it preparation or orchestration.

This lends itself to the essence of winning in a highly competitive world. With preparation, you become versed with the issues, and your reflexes are conditioned to deal with any anxieties and tensions.

There is no substitute for preparation. Preparation gives you the EDGE. Like running a marathon, being a better storyteller requires preparation; otherwise, things can fall apart. Here is how to gain the edge:

Enlist Help

Before the marathon (presentation) begins, you must reach within yourself and ask if you have the mental and physical resources to finish the race. If not, get a coach!

Plan Ahead

Here you have to design new possibilities for things that could go wrong. What if something goes wrong—what will you do to arrest the situation? What if things go right? How will you keep your focus so as not to get carried away if things don't work as planned during your presentation?

Grounded

To be grounded means to be real in your delivery. If the lights go off, will you acknowledge it or just continue with your rehearsed message? More importantly, how are you going to reach the goal of touching minds and hearts? To be grounded is to have a sense of where you are going, without getting distractor or destabilized by any minor "earthquake."

Back in 2004, I was doing a presentation on the topic of, "The Power of Preparedness," at a large health and safety conference at a University in Singapore. Just after presenting my first slide, the PowerPoint connection crashed. I was very nervous. By some twist of luck, I looked at the audience and said, "This is a true test of preparedness!" That little ad lib brought the house down with laughter. So I continued presenting without the PowerPoint slides for about 5 minutes before the issue was resolved. The adlib kept me grounded. Since that incident, I started collecting catchy one-liners to use whenever something unexpected happens. Turns out, nothing of that magnitude has happened lately.

Enduring

Enduring means you are willing to think long and hard about how long your message will take root in their hearts and minds. An enduring message does not happen by chance. It happens by careful consideration.

Conclusion:

In conclusion, it is important to observe high achievers in your field. If you want to be a high achiever in any field, be ready to pay the price. Quite often, the price is very high. It is as high as becoming an Olympian; it takes training, time, try-outs, coaching, equipment, injuries, mistakes, low moments, high moments, knockdowns, and knockouts, etc.

Three Ways to Apply Lessons Learned from This Chapter:

1. Use the Five Gs (5 Gs) of a Captivating Story

This ensures that you keep the story concise and engaging.

2. One Way to Deepen Your Connection with Your Audience

How can you demonstrate the Ubuntu concept in connecting with your audience?

3. The Titanium Rule

The Titanium Rule emphasizes individual connections and preferences. How can you use the Titanium rule to connect deeper with your story?

Part 2

Practical Ways to Capture The Hearts & Minds of Your Audiences

In this second part of the book, I have summarized frequently asked business storytelling questions from my workshop participants in over 10 countries. This format enables you to quickly find the answer you may need right away.

Chapter 4:

Concerns, Shortcuts, and Ways to Win Hearts and Minds: FAQ and Tips

Section 1: Concerns about structure and questions about Dynamic Storytelling

Question 1: How can I use a story to get my ideas and points across to the listening party?

Have you ever tried to explain a difficult concept to someone with limited knowledge? My mom once asked me, "What is the Internet?" I stuttered for an answer, especially because she did not have formal education. In other words, I had limited pre-existing references to draw upon.

That is where the importance of story comes in. A story is an experience shared to illustrate, clarify or influence someone. In the case of my mother, I told her that the Internet is an invisible information road network. I drew upon her pre-existing knowledge of the complex road network in our home city.

With that picture of the road network in her mind, I explained that instead of goods, the invisible network carries information via wires and cables. I also said that unlike the real world networks, the Internet is faster, and the information sent is received in a matter of seconds, worldwide.

"Ah that is so interesting. Now, I think I understand it for the first time," she said. That was very heartwarming to me. Without the mini-story and metaphor of a road network, it would have been very tough for me to convey the idea of the Internet to her.

I've used this example to show how you can use **a story as a bridge or a metaphor** to express your ideas, or share basic information with another party. The special advantage a story offers is that it enables you to engage both the mental and emotional faculties of your listener.

Thus, a well-told story gives you the unique opportunity to **frame or phrase** an issue in a way that is favorable to you. If you choose the wrong frame, your listener might not understand your idea well. On the other hand, if you choose a good frame, you can easily establish rapport with the listener.

If you want to excel in using storytelling, always take note of things that happen to you in life, and the lessons you learn from them. Consider keeping a journal with events, metaphors, and lessons learned. This is a powerful resource for frequent business use.

Question 2: How do I craft a story that sustains my audience's attention from start to finish?

For me, I try to craft business stories that capture both ordinary and extra-ordinary elements of our humanity.

My approach is inspired by the work of American mythologist, Joseph Campbell, famous for the book, "The Hero with a Thousand Faces."

Based on my understanding of Campbell's work that talks about the hero's journey (model), I believe that a riveting business story must have a mix and match of contradictory forces at work: good, evil, rise, fall, good guy, bad guy, mystery, victory, conflict, conscience, suspense, subtlety, mountains, valleys, virtue, vice, and so on. This creates a fluctuation in the emotional energy levels.

Without the ups and downs, the friends and foes, the darkness and light, a business story will be boring or mundane. In other words, a compelling business story must have positives and negatives. This is what makes it engaging and exciting.

Question 3: How do I find the right target audience to test my stories on before taking them to the main stage?

It is not always possible or practical to test a story in front of a large audience. For this reason, try out three practical alternatives: family and friends, social clubs, and open mics. The first two options are considered a safe-to-fly zone with minimum risk, while the third option is a no-fly or "fly-at-own risk" zone.

Family & Friends:

They are part of your captured audience. You can test your stories on them. One trick, however. Don't tell them at the start that you are testing. Ideally, you should only inform them after you've gotten some feedback. Don't expect any applause, let alone a standing ovation. Pay close attention to eyes and body response. Beware that friends and family can also be your harshest critics. Some may use this critique to get even about something else, so take it with a grain of salt.

Social Clubs:

Have you ever heard about an organization called Toastmasters? It promotes public speaking and leadership. Since 1924, it has been empowering its membership in several countries of the world. Clubs consist of about 20-50 members who meet weekly or monthly to support each other's growth. Having been a member for about eight years, I know this is a safe environment to test out new stories and get helpful feedback and input from my peers.

Open Mics: Welcome to the No-Fly, or Fly-at-Your-Own Risk Zone

In most cities worldwide, there are weekly "open mic" venues that host local talent shows for amateurs and professionals to try out new material. It differs from city to city. However, such events allow performers who range from poets, comedians, storytellers, singers, guitarists, etc., to perform for free. Each performer is given about five minutes to try out new material, or to improve upon old material.

Unlike testing with friends and family, or at social clubs, open-mics may have hecklers. Don't let this deter you. It does not happen regularly, based on my experience in the US and Singapore. Most major cities of the world have such venues. If you can conquer an open-mic, you'd do very well in a variety of settings.

In summary, I believe that you can get a bit creative in testing your stories. Once they are well prepared, sneak them into social conversations with friends, family, at social clubs, or open-mics. Ready-set-tell!

Question 4: How does one craft a good story without having had many powerful life experiences?

I believe one does not need to have had many earth-shattering life experiences to be able to tell a good story. A good story can come from everyday situations. If the storyteller has the skill and understanding, he or she can craft it well, and tell it well.

There are three ways to find good stories: autobiography, daily perks and quirks, and special wisdom.

Autobiographical Stories

You can derive or insource autobiographical stories by viewing your life from three parts; the early or the take-off years, the full flight, and landing years. During each phase, you ask yourself one question: "What are the three most important lessons that I have learned?" Each phase generally consists of about 15 years.

For each key lesson, craft a story about what happened, and how you came to discover the new lesson. It does not have to be story of climbing Mt Everest. It could be something as simple as playing chess.

Daily Quirks & Perks

Every day, we have little challenges, failures and surprises. In each of them, there is a story. What happened, who was involved, and what was the outcome? Was there any mystery or suspense involved? Those are the elements that you can capture in a story. Even a modest event works, such as falling on a wet floor, getting bitten by a cat, getting a scolding from your grandpa, and so on. All of these are relatable, and offer an opportunity to share a unique point of view. That is what makes a good story. It does not necessarily require a lot of drama to be interesting.

Folk Wisdoms and Intriguing Contemporary Anecdotes

An often-ignored source of good stories is the wisdom that circulates in contemporary literature or life lessons from folktales shared by grandparents, parents, uncles, aunts, and relatives. These are all rich sources of stories that you can draw from. They key is to give credit to your sources. Your challenge is to source, sort and find business lessons behind each story.

Consider this example from Malcom Gladwell‘s book, *Outliers: The Story of Success*. He writes that at the inauguration Benjamin Franklin ‘s statue in 1856, Robert Winthrop said, “Lift up your heads and look at the image of a man who rose from nothing, who owed nothing to parentage or patronage, who enjoyed no advantages of early education which are now open, - a hundred fold to yourselves, who performed the most menial services in the businesses in which his early life was employed, but who lived to stand before kings and died to leave a name which the world will never forget."

Finding and storing stories and anecdotes that intrigue you into a story bank is a fun exercise if you want to reduce your stress and anxiety levels when preparing for presentations and speeches that come up at short notice. I have scores of such anecdotes in my repertoire that I can draw from at short notice when I have time sensitive presentations.

Question 5: Must a story come from your own personal experience?

Based on my own experience and from general awareness, it is much better to use a personal story. This may not always be possible or practical, because you may have some complex issues that require third party stories or narratives.

Here are my thoughts on why I think that stories based on personal experience(s) are far more effective:

1. **You are the authority**. When the story is about you, you become the final authority on its authenticity. In other words, you don't open yourself up for unnecessary scrutiny from people who want you to fail professionally, i.e., your competitors.
2. **You can reenact the emotions**. Based on your personal sentiments and emotions felt during the incident, you can better reenact it to capture the attention of your audience. In other words, if

the story had happened to someone else, you can't fully examine his emotions and feelings.

3. **Credibility**. By telling your own story, you are enhancing your personal brand. This means that if the story becomes popular, your reputation grows. Credibility is a priceless asset in the marketplace today. It strengthens your likability and trustworthiness, which is not a bad investment.
4. **Signature story**. If a personal experience is well-told, and becomes a story by which you are recognized, and you have just found a signature story. Audiences crave such stories, and if yours is well received, you are well on your way to stardom on the speaking circuit.
5. **Ownership**. From conception to crafting and on to delivery, storytelling is a demanding process. If you persist though, and create a story that you are proud of, you have complete ownership of it, because nobody else can tell your story the way that you can tell it.

Thus, in essence, the value derived from a story well told about a personal experience far exceeds the value generated from telling another person's story, no matter how well it is crafted. So do yourself one favor today, and craft a story based on a personal experience.

Question 6: Why do you call storytellers gatekeepers?

Based on my observations, I believe storytellers are the moral gatekeepers of society. To play this role well, they act like movie directors who reenact (see and tell) through powerful images and characters combined. Their goal is to uplift by informing, encouraging and inspiring. It is a tough job. Thus, to my understanding, the word "gate" stands for "guard-on-duty," "absorber in chief," "toll-free filter," and "elixir-giver."

Guards-on-duty

Storytellers are the perfect gatekeepers, because they are always on duty in the laboratory of life. They monitor and observe what is happening all around them—watching for the good guys, the bad guys, and the unethical guys. It is a 24-hour job. No breaks, no downtime, no prep time. It's all about work.

Absorber-in-chief

By absorbing all the details of life, the gatekeepers are able to see certain patterns. They have the trained eye to absorb information and identify which objects are real, and which ones are just scarecrows. This process is intense, and it requires a lot of physical and mental power. Only a true and dedicated gatekeeper can withstand the pressures of this job.

Toll-Free Processor

Every single day, there are countless bits and pieces of information to be observed, analyzed and synthesized for meaning. Gatekeepers take pride in doing this, and also processing the information into more digestible stories and narratives that will resonate with their audiences. It is an enormous job to process all this for free to come up with engaging and uplifting stories.

Elixir-Man

Thanks to their craftsmanship, gatekeepers are able to craft memorable messages. As the moral compass of the people, they exert a lot of influence on what stories are told, and what elixir (sacred vine of life) everyday heroes personify in their daily struggles. Often, their stories become contagious and spread as social currency.

Question 7. How is it possible to identify a story with a unique point to express a simple lesson?

For myself, I tend to choose stories that will have a stronger resonance and yet make a point. By point, I mean that the story projects optimism, shows obstacles, invokes intrigue, has an element of novelty, and transcends stereotypical thinking.

Point

A good story must make a point that is clear and concise. By point, I mean a lesson that contains a thought-provoking question or statement that stirs the listener into some kind of action. Here is an example of a useful point: "He who gets the buzz gets the biz."

Obstacles

A story is more interesting when it has conflict or obstacles for the protagonist to overcome. This is like the fuel that helps a fire to burn. Without the fuel, the fire will be very weak. The stronger the odds, the more interesting the story will be. It is the writer's job to magnify the conflict without overwhelming the protagonist.

Insight

This refers to the perspective or point of view expressed by the storyteller. This is the filter through which he or she looks at the world. One point of view is tragedy. Another is comedy.

Novelty

The element of novelty helps the crafter or storyteller to introduce something new to generate curiosity and suspense in the mind of the listener. When this is done correctly, it keeps the listener glued to find out more details.

Transcend

This is the concise or succinct message of the entire story. Some people refer to this as the payoff and others as the moral of the story. Whatever name you call it, craft it to be memorable and show transcendence from darkness to light.

Question 8. What stories are good for a job interview?

I'd say purpose-driven stories that let the employer know who you are. There is nothing as liberating as finding your purpose and living it! I believe your purpose is tied to what Malcom Gladwell calls, "meaningful work."

Your Purpose

Your purpose is a reflection of what you want to be, or your present station along the way to that destination. Every day, I am seeking to refine and perfect my love affair for what I consider to be my purpose as a knowledge broker or educator. What is your purpose?

As an educator I believe I am doing meaningful work, because it gives me autonomy, challenge, and fulfillment to learn and share with others. This line of work also gives me a lot of personal resonance with those I meet and serve on my journey.

Recently, I stumbled on Hollywood producer Adam Leipzeig's five questions about purpose. I was elated to know that though we use different metaphors, we both mean the same thing. When you listen, observe, and analyze the echo of your voice, you can tell if your voice resonates. Is there harmony and symphony with the environment, or terror and cacophony?

Alternatively, you can use these five Ps below to better choose your professional, spiritual and personal direction in life:

Personal Ambition (Internal compass)

What do you want to do with your life? Do you feel drawn to some "destination" to do something special, somewhere?

Passion (Deep energy)

What makes you come alive? What makes you proud? If you can find meaningful work in that area, you'd be able to live your purpose.

People (Environment)

Who are the people that cherish you? Such people are part of your environment that brings out the best in you. They could be family, friends, clients, colleagues or associates. By forging relationships with them, they will refine your voice and its resonance.

Paucity (Tribulations)

What needs can you fill with your special gift(s)? This could be something that only you can do well. If you focus on it, your donation will outlive your duration.

Possibilities (Opportunities)

Who else can you serve? Go find that person. Where is the group? Go find them. Moses had to go to the mountain; the mountain did not come to him. So go find your mountain, today. Don't delay!

Conclusion

Once you've found your purpose, your life will never be the same again. You'll be set free! Thus, in answering an interview question, draw your inspiration from your five Ps, and position yourself better.

Section 2: How to Raise Your Prices with Effective Storytelling

"Stories are such a powerful driver of emotional value that their effect on any given object's subjective value can actually be measured objectively."

— *Joshua Glenn and Rob Walker*

The best way to raise the price of an item, a product, or service is to give it greater **significance.** Significance refers to the quality of being worthy of attention or importance. Back in 1999, I visited my former boss, Bob Drage, at his residence in one of the suburb of Pretoria, South Africa.

I recall him showing me around his compound. I will never forget one of the items he showed me, a door from the Union Building, i.e., the Presidency of South Africa. He said, "Gideon, this door is priceless. It was the door leading to Madiba's (Nelson Mandela's) office." He bought it during renovation, and he was evidently very proud of that door, as you can expect.

That door was made significant by its origin, purpose, history, and current place. To make the process of raising your prices easier based on significance, I have come up with an acronym EMOTE. By EMOTE, I mean portray value, ideally without theatrics.

E = Endear your audience or advocates to your product or service by sharing about the significance of the item to you. Do it respectfully, such that others find the comfort to share in your love for it.

M = Meaning is the key to life. Without meaning, our lives are vague. Your job as the storyteller is to show the meaning, the visible and invisible value of your items, products or services.

O = Offer to your audience the opportunity to experience it, i.e., to see, feel, touch, and enjoy the special item. This allows your advocates to see themselves in the picture, romancing that special item.

T = Tell or share some of the specs of the item or service. Here, historical facts, feats and factoids are important, because they will become social currency to the prospect or advocates.

E = Evoke, i.e., bring to the conscious mind. You can do this with pictures or words to arouse interest from nostalgia, memory, or feeling. Have you ever been to a typical Thai or Japanese restaurant? Enough said.

Rob Walker demonstrated how this works years ago, and published in the New York Times about his astonishing findings. Random items, such as coffee mugs, and toasters bought at garage sales for less than $1, were sold for over $46 on eBay. They items were displayed with fictitious stories.

If my math is correct, he saw profits of over a thousand percent. Not bad for a fictitious storyteller. Now, I don't encourage you to tell fictitious stories. I urge you to use authentic stories to engage and nudge your prospects, students, customers, and advocates to pay you more for what you are due.

Engaging with EMOTIONS

EMOTIONS	TRIGGERS	MANIFESTATION
Irritation	Pinch in shoe Negative feedback	Tension Scratch head
Frustration	Facebook picture Self guilt	Sigh Tension
Suspicion	Text message Eye contact	Walk off Look away
Shock	No bonus Retrenched	Outburst Voice trembles
Envy	Recoil Cringe	Curse Scoff

Section 3: Strategies to Cut through the Clutter

Question 1: How long should a story last before people lose interest?

In a business setting, a story should last on average three minutes. However, in a non-business setting, it can be longer. A story is like a song or an invisible instrument. When it is too long, people lose interest in it.

Before examining the significance of a three-minute business story, it is important to think about the purpose of the story. All stories are not born equal. Some are conceived to engage, while others are crafted to persuade or entertain.

Engaging Story:

If a story is aimed at introducing an issue or situation, you could choose an anecdote that engages audiences. In such a case, the story could be a minute long or less; after all, it is just meant to introduce an issue.

Persuasive Story:

Sometimes, the need arises to influence your audience. Such a story goes beyond engaging. Such a story could portray a hero who undergoes transformation, thanks to struggles that enable the hero to acquire a new understanding of life.

Entertaining Story:

An entertaining story can be both engaging and entertaining. Its primary goal is not to persuade. An entertaining story could be an embarrassing or self-deprecating experience.

Whatever type of story you choose, remember to craft it, and test it out to before taking it to the big stage. If you are serious about the quality of your story, know that you can't skip the element of writing and testing it carefully.

To sum it up, as a rule of the thumb, a business story should last about three minutes. A good story well-told can open doors that no Ivy League education can. Take your story very seriously.

Question 2: How can I tell my personal story in my business or social enterprise story?

It is possible to link your personal story to your business by showing how a personal frustration inspired a business solution. You can do this by first drawing your audience into your **igniting incident.**

An igniting incident is an incident or an experience that prompted the creation of your business. In this case, you created the business so that other people do not have to suffer the pain you did.

A while back, my friend's wife suffered a tragedy in Florida. While she was cooking dinner, her grandchild was playing behind the house. When she called the child for dinner and he did not respond, she went outside and found child floating in one of the open pools behind their house. The child had drowned. The lady was traumatized by this event for several months.

A few years after that incident, she decided to set up a foundation to educate other families to prevent such tragic incidents. She started a pool safety education programme for families in Fruitland Park, a small city, North of Orlando, Florida.

The **igniting incident** for her business was the drowning of the grandchild. Without that incident, she would not have been in that type of business. Thus, this tragic incident gave birth to the solution that now helps many families to prevent such painful accidents.

An igniting incident draws the audience in emotionally with a story that shows how a painful past leads to a hopeful future. Beyond the tragedy and trauma, show the connection or the link between the tragedy and the future. This is what gives the audience hope. Ideally, this earns sympathy, trust and hope for a better future. The stronger the connection, the more credibility you generate for your business or cause.

Out of the trauma of losing a grandson, a pool safety foundation was born to help other families to be safe and not sorry. That single statement bridges the personal and public, the past and the present. In other words, it transcends the pain of the past into a gain for the future.

Question 3: What are the most important considerations in using a story in a presentation?

There are several considerations; however, I can only address three here: relevance, circumstance, and significance. What do I mean by each of these?

Relevance

To determine if a story is relevant, ask this question: Is it related or important to the topic or key point? The relatedness or relevance could be viewed from a few angles, such as social, technical, historical, etc. If one of these conditions is present, you can assume that the relevance criterion is fulfilled.

If a story is relevant and useful in explaining a key point in your presentation, you can fine-tune it and use it in your presentation. Sometimes I run my relevance test through a few of my friends, who give me feedback. If they think the story is not highly relevant, I scrap it and find another one.

Circumstance

The circumstance element has to do with contextual meaning, or setting. Meaning relevance looks at the value; circumstance looks at the location. It evokes the relative position of the story to the issue.

When a story is told in the context of a key point, it enhances or strengthens the key point. On the contrary, if the story is not related and not in context, you should leave it out of the presentation. The key point is the surface, while the story adds to the substance.

Significance

Significance has to do with meaning and implications, or outcomes. A story that shows the outcome or results is a winner, because it enables the teller to win over any skeptics or cynics in the audience. To show significance, use both logic and emotions.

If the outcome that is important to the audience is financial, then the story should ideally have some numbers, percentages or figures that indicate trends or return on investment (ROI). On the other hand, if the outcome the audience wants is inner peace, a story that evokes that will also be very impactful.

There is an old adage in professional speaking circles that says, "Make a point and tell a story." It is very simple but poignant. Choose stories that have relevance, circumstance and significance. When you do that, your audience will eat out of your hands because you have what it takes to quench their thirst and nourish their soul.

Question 4: How do you make a story captivating and yet relatable?

A captivating and relatable story is one that resonates with the audience, getting it to embrace a new idea or concept. Below are six ways to make your stories more relatable.

Compelling Message

Relatable stories are crafted to teach a relatable message from carefully selected facts, factoids, and feats. Such stories are designed to be insightful by focusing on single issue, as opposed to too many.

Contemporary

Another key element is that such a story leverages current issues to make the message stick. The use of a current crisis anchors the story emotionally in the minds of the listeners.

Wired to Emotional Issues

This can be done by revealing a new trajectory or approach to solving a difficult problem. When done well, it becomes symbolic, and inspires action. One example is a story that encourages breastfeeding and shuns formula milk.

Casting

An ideal relatable story casts the community as a hero. By so doing, the audience feels empowered by the liberating role the hero plays. In this case, the storyteller becomes a mentor.

Resonance

Resonance is power. It is the energy or payoff the listener receives. The stronger the resonance, the further the story travels. Occasionally, there is an echo, or buzz, that is generated from a story.

Compass

Last, but not least, relatable stories must be noteworthy. This means that the listener experiences an intellectual or emotional shift that opens a new window of understanding about life, thanks to the story.

Question 5: What makes a good story, and how can a business story be used to move a customer along the sales funnel?

As humans, we are naturally sympathetic to a good guy's desires. We root for good guys to succeed, and for bad guys to fail. We root for the underdog. To make it interesting, give the good guy a worthwhile goal, like pursuit of a job to feed his family, paying off a debt, or getting out of jail to help a child in school. Noble goals are relatable. They also serve as a hook, i.e., keeping the audience engaged in finding out the outcome.

Goliath Antagonizes the Good Guy

After revealing the good goal, don't make it too easy for the good guy. Throw in a couple of bad guys to mount a series of roadblocks to impede the good guy. These obstacles or detours add intensity to the story. They also make it more interesting and intriguing.

Grueling Conflict Ensues

In writing the story, don't make the mistake of NOT casting your protagonist with some human flaws. His failures and shortcomings will make him or her more relatable. In other words, you don't need to sanitize your character(s); otherwise, they won't be credible to your audience

Guru Comes to Settle

The essence of a story is to educate, persuade or entertain. Thus, use your story to teach or transfer important life lessons to others. The guru is the one that delivers new meaning that helps the protagonist to see a new reality. He helps to get resolution.

Gift

Good storytelling starts with a good premise (idea), and ends with a good payoff or reward that inspires a listener to be a better person in life. It is also called the moral of the story. As you present the story, ask yourself if you have covered the five Gs:

- Good guy with a goal
- Goliath

- Grueling fight
- Guru
- Gift

Second Part of Question

Business stories are used to build awareness, credibility and trust to lubricate the process of buying. Stories ease that process so that it is not dry or jarring.

I assume you are aware of the sales funnel. Ideally, you should choose a story that is suitable for your prospect, i.e., his or her level of readiness. For a prospect that has already been exposed to you, an awareness story, like a magnetic story, is not ideal. Further down the funnel, it is better to share a mission, mayhem, or mastery story. **Check out chapter 2 for types of stories.**

Question 6: Where can I find compelling stories to use in everyday life or business situations?

There are five places to find compelling and personable stories for daily use or business purposes You can embed stories into your social or professional conversations as examples or illustrations. When they are used as examples, you can never go wrong. The reason is that everyone will see your story as an aid, not as a strategic tool. That is the catch! Here are a few places where you can find and use stories in daily personal or business life:

Personal Experiences

Every day interesting, disgusting, and unique events happen. Some teach important life lessons. The lessons learned from these experiences can be used in framing business concepts. So can you collect and curate these stories for business use? You can start a Story Catalogue today. This is a simple spreadsheet of stories.

Friends and Family

Once in a while, your friends and family members share some compelling stories or experiences that get you completely mesmerized. When that happens, make a note of it. If it is a remarkable incident, consider getting their permission to use it in the future as a business metaphor.

Professional Colleagues & Resources

Occasionally, your professional colleagues will share stories from their work or family life. Some of these stories can be so unique that you regale your own family with the tales from your colleagues. Such stories can also be used in business settings, with suitable credit given to the sources.

Customers, Mentors & Founders

Stories about customers, mentors, and founders can be very effective in business settings because they are symbolic. Ideally, customer, mentor, or founder stories are used in communicating with other customers or employees; however, they can also be used for other reasons, including instruction and persuasion.

Business Trips

When you travel, make a note of things that happen, like missing a flight, losing luggage, or facing a blackout in foreign country. Such incidents are unique, yet relatable. With some exploration, each of them teaches a lesson that can be used as a business analogy.

Generally, audiences connect better with stories of a personal nature, so remember to use such stories, because they will have a stronger resonance with your audience(s).

Question 7: Is there ever too much of a good thing where business storytelling is concerned?

Is there a point at which the use of storytelling in business is excessive and becomes overkill? You should ask the prospect, “Do you mind if I share with you what happened to me?” If you get permission, you reduce the burden of making this mistake. Second, if you make the judgment that you have used too many examples or stories, it is time to use some other form of persuasion like physical demonstration.

Question 8: How do I choose which message to present to my audience?

I’d say it all depends on whether you are speaking to the Eskimos of Greenland or the Bushmen of the Kalahari Desert. Do you want to be known as the guy who sold snow to the Eskimos? That’s like selling a mongongo nut to the Bushmen. You get the point.

Just like trainers do a Training Needs Analysis, I believe that as a business storyteller you need to do some kind of internal need analysis to figure out what the audience would be receptive to. One way to do this is do a DNA analysis, something I do for every speech. What does it stand for?

Distressing Issues:

This is something you identify that is stressing out the audience. By coining a message that reflects their pain, it shows sympathy. It tells them, "I care."

Needs:

If you can figure out what they need and what inspires them, you can better present a message that reassures or encourages them to reach their destination.

Aspirations:

What is it that they want to see practically in their lives? What kind of outcome? By addressing these aspirations, you give them the opportunity to take a deep breath, knowing that you know what they want.

Question 9: Must stories be told in an animated and interesting way?

There are perhaps three ways to look at this question: animated delivery, a zero-animated delivery, and a moderately animated way of delivery. I'd like to examine each of them, and let you make your choice. Before exploring each, it is worthwhile mentioning that the degree of animation may also depend on the purpose and audience.

The Case for Animated Delivery

Storytellers who are very animated tend to use a lot of physicality in their delivery. Others may use a lot of props in combination with body language to get their message across. Three famous celebrities who have used this type of delivery quite often are: Robin Williams, Jim Carrey and Anthony Robbins.

The Case for Zero-Animation

There is hardly any famous actor or speaker that uses zero animation in the perfect sense of its definition. Perhaps the closest examples are Mother Teresa, Dalai Lama, and Pope Benedict XVI. It may be unfair to include the Dalai Lama's name, because he often bows a lot and uses facial expressions in telling.

The Case for Moderate Animation

Moderate use of animation in storytelling implies that animation is used when required, and not used when there is no need. The vast majority of storytellers fall into this category. Prominent examples would be Whoopi Goldberg, Michelle Yeow, and Jackie Chan.

No style is perfect. It depends on the storyteller's personality and the audience. Some storytellers are physical when telling stories to kids. Others only use animation to make their points clearer and more effective.

Thus, in essence, it is better for the individual to go with what suits his personality. That way, the delivery will be smooth. Each style offers something unique, and I believe each storyteller can benefit from picking up tools from the other style.

Question 10. How do I overcome fear when making a presentation?

I believe fear is a double-edged sword. If you manage it well, it can work in your favor. Thus, the big question is, how can you turn this destabilizing state of mind into an empowering presence on stage? There three ways you can use to transcend stage fright: pre-event prep, mental prep, and physical exercises.

Pre-Event Preparation

Each time I have not prepared sufficiently for a presentation, I tend to have some jitters. The less prepared I am, the stronger the jitters. Thus, I believe it is very important to be self-assured that you have put in the best preparation time you can before the event, because this will minimize the jitters.

Mental Preparation

Before a humorous speech contest last December, I was very nervous. It did not help that I was the first speaker. Ouch! In the midst of that chilly moment of fright before facing 700 people in the room, I stepped away from the crowd. I went into a room back stage.

There I sat down, away from the noise, to meditate. I used a system called rhythmic breathing: breathe in for four seconds, hold for four seconds, and then breathe out for four seconds. It takes a minimum of four rounds. I recall that I did three rounds, forcing myself to ignore every distraction. Fortunately, it calmed me down and quelled my nerves. Only then I was ready to face crowd.

Physical Exercises

Other speakers I know do moderate physical exercises, such as body stretches, to dissolve their nerves backstage. Recently, I read about some research from Colombia University. It indicates that your posture, gestures, and smile can also affect your stage fright. A simple facial expression, like a smile, can induce confidence within.

It reduces the stress-inducing hormones cortisol and adrenaline. One study found that using gestures improves the brain's coordination with hands in producing speech during delivery. So is the case with other confidence-inducing postures such as the Super Woman pose, Oprah's signature pose, or the arms akimbo position (hands are on the hips and the elbows are bowed outward, or bent)

In summary, to overcome fear during a presentation, you can rehearse thoroughly before the event, meditate, or use moderate physical exercises just before walking onto the stage.

Question 11. How do I use stories to articulate my vision and mission when speaking to stakeholders?

Suppose you are a construction company, how would you empower your employees to offer their best so that your company can be one of the most sought after in the country? How can you express your mission of being the best to your employees, such that they take pride in their daily work to help you reach that goal?

Simply telling them that your company, "XYZ Company, is the industry leader," is subjective and vague. It does not move your team to go the extra mile in their work. One way to do that is tell a story that casts your employees as heroes in what they do, no matter how small it may be.

There is an analogy that runs loosely as follows. One morning, an old lady was out for a walk. She ran into a group of men working at a construction site. She asked one of them, "What are you doing?" Angrily, one of the man replied, "Can't you see I am laying bricks?"

She was baffled. Then she walked over to the second man, and asked him the same question. The man looked up, smiled, and politely said, "Madam, I am laying bricks that will be used in constructing the best cathedral in this city."

The old lady thanked him, and walked off. She thought to herself, "What a difference an appreciation of one's job can make!" The second man's response was very refreshing. He seemed to be proud of his work, very engaged, and focused.

Who do you think had a copy of the business's mission and vision statement? Who do you think had both the statement and a full story (picture) of the significance of his job? Perhaps the first guy only had a copy of the mission and vision statement read to him.

On the other hand, it appears that the second guy had a bigger picture or narrative about the significance of his work, and he knew he was a part of the big picture of a top company. This somewhat simple analogy demonstrates that a story can do a better job of helping an employee to feel engaged, take pride in his work, and feel that he is part of a bigger entity.

A mission or vision statement is a crisp and concise statement that embodies a lot of meaning. For it to be brought to life, leaders need to tell stories that breathe life into the dead or stoic statement.

Question 12: How can I tell the story behind the origin of my social enterprise or business?

The story behind your business is what I call the backstory, or igniting incident. It is the story that separates you from anyone else in the same line of business. Some authors call it the genesis story, the origin story. Whatever name you call it, I believe you should tell it to capture the imagination of your audience.

It is your job to do three things: draw the audience into the scene, help them to appreciate what is at stake, and then show them the silver-lining.

So how do you draw the audience into the scene? Craig Valentine, the1999 World Champion of Public

Speaking, talks about VAKS, an acronym for "visual," "auditory," "kinesthetic" and "smell." VAKS helps you to fully engage and immerse your audience. It awakens their senses of sight, hearing, touch, and smell.

When this is done well, it enables the audience to connect deeper with you sensually. They get to feel your the pain, your fears and the frustration you experienced. This serves to underlie the importance of why you decided to take action, i.e., to avoid similar pain in future.

Further, you also need to help the audience see what is at stake. Is a career or family at stake? By painting this picture, the audience gets to see and feel the impact of action or inaction. You can do this by highlighting the moral or ethical implications, and the urgency of taking action now.

End by showing the silver-lining behind the very dark clouds of that experience. Ideally, the silver-lining is the business or cause you are championing. By casting your business as the solution, you are inevitably asking the audience to come join you in defeating the forces of darkness that have besieged your world.

At its very core, the story behind your business shows a broken world that only your business can repair. In other words, your business is the protagonist that wants to take the risk to heal a broken world. When you do that well, the world will beat path to your door. I think this is how Martin Luther King and Steve Jobs did it.

Question 13: How can I leverage the power of stories to differentiate and energize my business or my brand?

Storytelling is a great brand differentiator. It energizes and electrifies a business beyond physical borders. Story evangelists tell stories that precede products. Quite often, the footprint of a story is wider than that of a product or service. That footprint comes from the energy generated through buzz.

Even though there is power in a story, that power must be plugged in for it to flow to the users. So it is your job to craft and tell (plug in) compelling stories that come with hidden electricity. **PLUG** is an acronym. It stands for then **Four Ways Your Story Differentiates You,** thanks to the voltage it carries within.

- Paint the future
- Laden with electricity
- Unveil the past
- Gift

Paint the future:

In a well-crafted story, you can communicate your values and your vision for the world. Everyone has a story to tell. Unfortunately, not everyone is telling his story. A well-told story is like a futuristic painting that is uplifting.

Laden with electricity:

These are stories designed to entertain, inform, influence or inspire. The inner genius of story is that it does not influence coercively in a brash way. It gets into your mind, and slowly, like a Trojan horse, takes over, thanks to framing. Without framing, a story will lose all its brilliance or potent electricity.

Unveil the past

One type of story that is least often used is a backstory. It is great at eliciting empathy. It taps into the past, to earn empathy by espousing noble goals. When this is done correctly, the teller earns goodwill and support from the audience. A company without a good backstory is like a car without steering.

Gift

A well-told story ends with a lesson that crystalizes a point, learned or desired. By harnessing that lesson and sharing it, you are giving the listener the very best of your journey or learning. When this happens, that lesson becomes a form of energy or electricity that travels from mouth to mouth, mind to mind, and heart to heart.

It is the ultimate currency of human contact. It is capable of differentiating your brand or business, because no two companies have the same exact currency, purchasing power, past, vision, values, or the voltage of connection.

Question 14: How can my business get closer to clients worldwide by using storytelling effectively?

Effective storytelling enables your business to benefit by developing a stronger connection, differentiation, and retention in the minds of customers. About 81% of clients search online before making a purchase. There is a good chance that your prospects are checking you out online.

Do you want to stand out? Do you want to be memorable and different from the other myriad of websites online today? That is where your story comes in, because everyone's story is different.

Connection

Perception is reality, they say. This means if a local or global client makes contact with your business online, if your story is well-written, this increases the chances for your prospect to develop an emotional connection or an interest in your company.

Thus, in crafting your story, pay attention to your backstory, because it enhances the possibility of your prospects liking you, and to start rooting for you to succeed. Have you ever rooted for a character in a movie? A well-crafted story about the founder gets the prospect to root for your success.

Differentiation

By differentiation, I mean that your story enables you to stand out from all other companies providing similar services like yours. A well-written story humanizes your company. It makes the prospect feel that you're real, and not just a faceless, ruthless, moneymaking machine. When you humanize and humorize, you surprise your prospect, because organizations don't do that today. One good way to humanize is to share a bit about the lives of the people behind the products, keeping it real.

Retention

A few minutes after a client visits your website, will he still remember you? Was there something about you that was unique and memorable? Neurological studies show that our brains remember stories more, because they help us to make sense of life. In crafting your story, drop in bits and pieces of "social currency," i.e., unique facts that are easy to remember and use in a conversation. *"Do you know that Singapore went from third world to first in one generation?"* That's an example of social currency!

Question 15: When do you inform your clients of the price during a story? How can you use storytelling to increase lead generation?

Do you like pushy salesmen? I prefer someone who gives me space to make up my mind. It allows me to reflect. Thus, my answer here is more about sharing, not selling. I believe if you do a good job sharing, the selling comes by itself. It is the backbone of my business. I have never taken a sales class, but I have taken countless story classes.

Besides being subtle and gentle, stories allow you to share your Point of View (POV) in a non-invasive way. That is a beautiful thing. Why is that powerful, you may ask. To me, every POV is different and unique.

The next time you have to sell something, step back and find a compelling story. Share it as an experience by highlighting your POV, and the key point of your story (POS). The POV frames the discussion, and the POS tames the conversion.

Show them the Future

This means you paint a picture with a metaphor or a symbol that is desirable. You can't paint a great picture unless you have great ideas, experiences and tools. That is why sharing is better than selling. Consider this provocative example from Las Vegas or Sin City: "What happens in Vegas stays in Vegas."

Hold on to Higher Values

This is noble and respectful of the other person's own values. Don't coerce or diminish others. Share yours. Give an example of a time you took the highroad. The highroad takes you beyond the crossroads. Think about Nike's "*Just do it!*" It is a mini story. It is less than six words, but very inspiring; it sells a higher value.

Abate their Fears

With a good story, you can reduce tension, and come clean of the past. This enables you to mitigate any bad air that engenders resentment. By abating turmoil, you alleviate the tensions, which show you are in control.

Redress to Reform

You can rekindle a soured relationship by sharing a story that sows new seeds. This conjures a new beginning.

It also redresses any distress. This is possible because when you reform, you renew.

Emodutain and Elevate

Edutainment wraps critical information (education) with entertainment. It is a Trojan horse strategy. It works because it gets the subject to switch off, laugh, and relax. When that happens, they are more inclined to accept what you offer, because they are on a higher acceptance and bonding curve, which breeds consensus and harmony. Through the pleasure, you can communicate the painful.

Next Step

Try three of the above strategies and see what happens. Then Email me at Gideon@1xtramile.com to let me know which you chose and how it worked for you. Thank you. Alternatively, if you have been using stories extensively, feel free to share some of your successful stories. I'd be delighted to share with my audiences and credit you.

Question 16: What is a good story to tell when everyone is frustrated or confused in a meeting?

In this type of situation, use a story as a metaphor. You could start by saying, "Our current situation reminds me of a problem I faced in Istanbul, Turkey in 2012, a problem Pablo Picasso faced with the Romans in 1948, a situation Jackie Chan faced encountered in the movie Rush Hour 3, at the Eiffel Tower in France. The idea here is to be specific, so it gets everyone thinking.

The novelty of a specific situation gets everyone's attention, out of curiosity. In their minds, they are wondering, how did the Romans solve such a problem? From that moment, match the emotional mood of the audience before moving it to a higher state of meaning. In other words, meet and match before you move. First, you must meet them where they are, match the mood and energy emotionally with empathy, before slowly moving them to a higher plateau or plane of influence. When you do that, you demonstrate empathy as one of them. When this is done, you have earned a bit of leverage to then move or uplift them to a higher platform, involving entertainment, inspiration or empowerment.

Thus, in essence, first you calm their nerves, and when you have earned their confidence, you can then take them somewhere else. Select a good story, depending on the collective state of mind of your audience. If they are very sad, share a story that resembles their situation, and then go from there.

Question 17: Should the story be full of suspense so that people will become more interested?

To a large extent yes; however, you must know that suspense is not the only desirable quality of a good story. You have many literary devices that you can use. Suspense helps you get keen listeners to listen in. Some will be glued in. That is good. But if you overdo it, they may switch off.

Another consideration is that the amygdala, the brain's radar, likes suspense. The amygdala determines which activity is important and which is not; hence, it determines whether the rest of the brain is engaged or not. Use your suspense wisely, i.e., not to the point of creating suspense fatigue.

Three Ways to Apply Lessons Learned in this Chapter

1. **Five Ps of Purpose**
   Use the five Ps of Purpose as a guiding light; when your stories are tied to purpose, your authenticity shines through.

2. **Tell or Pitch With Passion**
   Without passion, you come across as passive. Your audience feeds on your energy.

3. **Resonance**
   Resonance is power. Observe your resonance based on ECHO, i.e., **E**xpressions like smiles, **C**laps, **H**ead nods, and **O**ohs and ahs.

Chapter 5:

Secret Ways to Capture the Hearts & Minds of Prospects, Customers & Advocates

Section 1: Secret: How to Use the NISS Formula to Penetrate the Mind Like a Trojan Horse

The NISS Approach

When choosing a story to share, pick one that is captivating and memorable with respect to the NISS qualities. NISS is steeped in neuroscience research. It has to do with the way the amygdala, i.e., the gatekeeper to the brain, works. I have crafted the NISS formula based on the work of several A-List neuroscience academics.

Novelty - The amygdala hates monotony, and pays attention to something new.

Intrigue - The human mind likes to figure out the missing pieces to a puzzle.

Specificity - The brain is capable of remembering specific details such as red kayak.

Surprise - The element of surprise or suspense is consummately engaging.

Novelty

The human mind craves novelty. Something new, something shiny and different will be more engaging and memorable, as opposed to something mundane.

I believe this accounts for why the movie industry has an obsession for creating new, weird and memorable characters such as Superman, Batman, and Shrek. Because these characters are new and different, they tend to be more memorable.

Intrigue

A good story needs an element of myth. When there is something amiss, the audience leans forward, trying to understand, or to find the missing piece of the puzzle. The human loves to find the answer; this explains why crossword puzzles and Sudoku are very popular.

Surprise

An element of surprise, or the unexpected, adds to freshness of a tale. It also keeps the audience anticipating when the next surprise is going to happen. Was there an ambush? When there is, there occurs an adrenalin rush in the mind of the reader or the audience. Not only is it engaging, it also increases neurological activity and enhances memory retention, according to some research conducted by Dr. Larry Cahill, of University of California, Irvine.

Specifics

When telling a story, be very specific. This will allow listeners to see pictures in their minds, and remember what you are talking about. In other words, instead of talking about staying at a hotel in Dubai, talk about staying at Hotel 81 in Dubai. That specificity goes a long way in shaping the mind.

Prune the Hedges and Pave the Road

When you foresee objections, hesitation, or outright rejection, you need a story that prunes down the hedges to help your team to forge ahead. Have you watched the movie The Great Debaters, starring Denzel Washington? Much of the pep talk in that film falls within this category of using either prose or poetry to prune down or reduce the barriers.

In essence, what you address in such a movie are the obstacles, and how to get through them; the hedges, and how to leap over them. When this is done through narrative, it allows the listener to dream a new dream, to see a different picture, and to find ways to beat or defy the odds.

Section 2: Stop Selling, Start Sharing

Do you like pushy salesmen? I prefer someone who gives me space to make up my mind. It allows me to reflect. That is very respectful. What about you?

The next time you have to sell something, step back and find a compelling story. Share it as an experience by highlighting your POV (Point of View) to give your audience the benefit of your perspective. Your POV provides depth and value to the issue under consideration.

1. Shape the Future

To shape the future, describe that future to someone. Use pictures and metaphors to bring it closer. You need to have great ideas and past experiences to shape the future. When you do this well, the picture is clearer, and people begin to line up.

2. Handle Objections

This is noble, and respectful of the other person's own values. Don't coerce or diminish others. Share your point of view by using a story. Give an example of a time you took the highroad. That will speak for itself.

3. Attract Attention

With a good story, you can level the playing field. Even the best-trained Ivy League graduates will have no chance against you. Politely tell your well-polished story, and watch the room shift in your favor. I've seen prepared storytellers from mushroom schools bring back the room to life after a boring, C-suite speaker from the Ivy-League put them to sleep.

When audiences see a good storyteller, they sit up, listen, enjoy the entertainment, and then start tweeting, sharing and talking about the speaker right from there. That builds buzz and gets attention from potential prospects.

4. Raise Prices

Random items bought from garage sales were resold, with embellished stories, at an over 2700% increase in price via eBay. Items that were bought for $.90 to $1.20 were resold for over $40 per item, thanks to fictitious stories that humanized the items, and made them look like special artifacts or storied items.

5. Emodutain

Edutainment wraps critical information with entertainment and emotional engagement. That means powerful views or ideas are buried within humorous and humanizing tales or fable. It works because of the packaging, i.e., a seemingly benign and tame facade.

Section 3: Build Trust and Respect with Mayday Stories

A Mayday story shows how you've survived a tribulation, a trying moment in your life. Crucible stories are particularly useful in shifting perspectives, because they reveal unexpected, humbling situations in which a hero could have sold out, but instead of taking the easier route, the hero persisted to the end. It reveals character, audacity, and grit.

These are qualities that are limited today. By sharing a story of how you avoided immediate gratification—the easier route, your audience gets a sense you are someone it can trust, someone whose character has been formed through blood, sweat, tears, and soot.

A good Mayday story captures a crucible moment or two. It should show how someone helped you to survive, not you doing it all by yourself. This humanizes the experience, and draws in your audience, because others picture themselves exasperated in that same tough place.

It helps the listener to gain a new perspective about life. It shows how you transcended, and how others can learn from you. It shows how you went from grief to relief or from pitfall to windfall!

So how do you find crucible moments?

Begin by looking at what I call "**The Six Phases of life.**" Each phase is 15 years. The first phase is called the **Dependency Phase.** The next 15 years are the **Taxing Phase.** Beyond the age of 30 is referred to as the **Take-off Phase.** After age of 45, you have the **Full Flight Phase.** Beyond 60, you enter the **Descent Phase and 75 years,** you get into the **Landing Phase**

0 -15 Dependency Years

15 -30 Taxing Years

30 - 45 Take-off

45 - 60 Full Flight Years

60 - 75 Descent Years

75 ++ Landing Years

From each phase, you can find the lowest and highest moments. What did you learn from the low moments, or drifts? That's where the crucible magic or the best wisdom lies. If you had to crystallize the best you learned from those moments and tell an eight-year-old child, what would you say?

I tend to use what I call the "**Shift**" analysis to capture the lessons from the lowest and highest moments of my life. Shift is an acronym that reminds me of what I must do to derive a compelling story:

- Synthesize
- Highlight
- Insight
- Feelings and
- Touch-point

Here is a synopsis of what each word stands for.

Synthesize

Identify a personal experience that you thought was an important lesson. Use it to show a turning point in your life, during which you were powerless, and yet it turned out well.

Highlight

Beyond the turning point, highlight how it felt being vulnerable. Be as specific as possible: time, place, words, images, thoughts, cravings, etc. Use sensory details. What could you see, smell, hear, or feel?

Insight

Offer your point of view (POV) about the incident or event. The point of view helps the listener see the world through your eyes. It draws the audience to your side, with empathy. Without this, you've not added value.

Feelings

If you want your audience to feel your pain, show it through your voice and tone. By doing this, you are conveying the true you, as humanly possible. It x-rays authenticity. It is of very high value, because it can either engage or repel or your listener.

Touch-point

Touch-point means, the lesson you learned that you could pass along. In other words, you turn pain (pitfalls) into profit (windfalls). As the saying goes, "That which doesn't't kill you makes you stronger." When you pack it in such sound bites, it becomes memorable, quotable, and if you are lucky, Tweetable.

In summary, by utilizing the touch-point, you can help someone learn or benefit from your past to have a better future. What's your crucible story?

Three Ways to Apply Lessons Learned from this Chapter

Mine the Six Phases for Epic Stories

1. Think through your first phase, and identify one emotionally-charged or humorous story.
2. Think through your second phase, and identify an inspiring or embarrassing story you can tell to

generate curiosity or build rapport with a prospect or an audience.

3. Apply the SHIFT concept in crafting and polishing each of the stories and start testing in the safe zones.

Chapter 6:

How to Pitch and Nudge with Stories that Win Hearts & Minds

Section 1: How to Pitch with Stories

If you have an idea, a product, concept, or service you need to promote, you need a story to nudge people forward. Pitching is the ultimate test of your ability to convince and persuade someone to take action. If you want to pitch and be memorable, use a story anchored with props, if possible.

Whether it's formal pitching or not, the better prepared you are the better for you. Here are some steps you can take into consideration. One of the reasons pitches fail is that the presenters fail to hitch the audience. This is an inherent human condition that requires a better understanding of how the brain works.

The part of the brain that crafts critical pitch messages is the neocortex, i.e., the more sophisticated part of the brain that is capable of analyzing big concepts. However, the amygdala within the crocodile brain that receives pitches is not very smart. It is primarily responsible for safety, and not the sophisticated thoughts of the neocortex.

It is more concerned about survival issues. Thus, any information that is not new and interesting is ignored. Acting as the gatekeeper, the amygdala has very low tolerance for complex information or any form of complexity. If you fail to by-pass the gatekeeper, you will not get to the decision maker, the neocortex.

To outmaneuver the croc brain, you must give him something fresh and new, for he craves novelty or something that is not threatening.

The midbrain is concerned with social context. First, in crafting your pitch, you must find a way to hitch or bypass the amygdala in the croc brain before your pitch will get favorable attention by way of logical, analytical consideration in with the neocortex. Here are five ways to hitch before you pitch:

Hooking with Novelty

By this I mean that you must find something unique—different, but not threatening, or else the low attention croc brain will not bother. If the croc brain is interested, it communicates this urgency to the neocortex to take over.

Present an Intriguing Idea

Start with an engaging and intriguing idea that stimulates interest. Such an idea will build a bridge to the next idea. You can do this by using a little mystery or talking about a missing puzzle. This will generate a bit of creative suspense, something that the human brain loves to figure out.

Keep it Simple

Keeping it simple and avoiding complexity helps the croc brain to understand it without too much difficulty. If you want to pitch a very sophisticated concept, simplify it with an anecdote or a metaphor. This can go a long way.

Know Their Expectations

Before you pitch, try to anticipate where your audience is coming from, i.e., their fears and aspirations. This will enable you to earn or gain their full attention and appreciation in terms of your solution. You do this by framing your story and solution in terms of their needs and aspirations.

Show Benefits & Rewards

Last but not least, you need to show the audience the rewards or benefits. This will activate dopamine, a chemical that sends messages about pleasure. This creates a good feeling that relaxes your audiences to let them be fully tuned in.

Most of what is expressed above can be done with a carefully crafted series of stories that frame and reframe the issues in your favor. It is worth noting that for pitching to be effective, it must begin with hitching, and hitching can be enhanced significantly with a compelling story. Once that is done, the rest is easier.

Section 2: How to Move Them with Words: Lessons from One of the Greatest Introverted Orators

Lincoln - Master Crafter and Wordsmith

Having read several books about Lincoln and his personal charm, his storytelling and his charismatic personality, I am yet in awe of what I found in Donald T. Philips's *Lincoln on Leadership*. I came away with five important lessons to share with you.

Lesson # 1: An Introvert Can Make an Outstanding Public Speaker

In his youth, Abraham Lincoln was an introvert; however, as he grew up, he embraced storytelling and oratory. He did not give himself any excuses not to learn this skill just because he was an introvert. If you want to be a good or great public speaker, do not give yourself any excuses. Step up and learn this craft. You never know how far this will take your career.

Lesson # 2: The Extemporaneous Telling of a Story Must Be Practiced

One of the hallmarks of Lincoln's ability was thoroughness at preparation. He once said, "Extemporaneous speaking must be practiced and cultivated." Not only did he spend hours, days, and weeks preparing for his speeches, but he also never considered any single word or sentence done until delivered.

Do you rehearse what you say at important meetings? If a master of Lincoln's stature did it, it is certainly an indispensible part of getting ready to deliver a memorable presentation.

Lesson #3: Telling Your Story is a Continuous Journey

Eloquence and oratory in oral communication is like any other skill. It is honed over time. It takes time and effort. The famous "House Divided" speech given at the Republican State Convention in Springfield in 1858 is said to have been the most carefully **written and tested** speech of his life. What does this tell you about how much work you need to do to raise your game?

Lesson #4: Speaking Can Make or Break Your Career

On February 27, 1860, Mr. Lincoln gave what was perhaps the most important speech of his political career at the Cooper Institute in New York. He was venturing out to the East from Illinois, and he did not want to fail his audience. He worked on the speech for over three months, researching his facts and choosing his wording. Thanks to that speech and the press, he became famous out in the East.

Do you research thoroughly for your speeches and stories? You can't afford to overlook this critical element of engaging and moving your audience.

Lesson #5: A Speaker Dies, but His Ideas Live On

Thanks to his ability to speak well, his oratory, his storytelling and humor, we still remember Lincoln today. He has earned a special place in our hearts and minds. He was probably not the smartest president, but he certainly used oral communication to carve out a spot for himself in world history.

Think about how you can earn a place in the hearts and minds of your audience. You don't have to be the smartest, but you can be the most memorable person, who left a lasting impact.

Section 3: How to Move Them with Passion and Emotions, Not Coercion: Lessons from One of the Greatest Orators

Since 1993, I have read every single book or document that I have found about Martin Luther King, Jr. One that I found particularly useful is Donald T. Phillips's *Martin Luther King, Jr.* It was less focused on biographical elements, and more on critical elements of his leadership and communication style. The book taught me some salient points about his power of oratory as a tool for moving these followers.

1. Win by Persuasion, not Coercion or Alienation

During his career, Martin Luther King, Jr. used the power of story and persuasion to win over enemies, cynics, and bigots on the civil rights cause. Besides speaking to large crowds, he also took a lot of time to write individual letters to the people who did not agree with him.

After receiving a letter from a lady who stated that Negroes could never be equal to whites, MLK wrote back saying: "I must confess, I am in total disagreement with your position. This, however, does not at all cause me to hate those that believe in segregation." It appears that each and every single person who was persuaded mattered a lot to MLK. Can you use this in the design of your stories and messages? Everyone counts!

2. Seek to Understand Before you Speak

As a leader, Martin Luther King, Jr. sought the truth about issues before he spoke about them in public. He held the view that not all that is written is true. As a result, he often went out to the field to seek the facts, sent aides to obtain facts about burning issues, or made telephone calls to get firsthand information to inform his speaking. Can you find some inspiration in this approach to speaking that is fueled by a desire to first seek the facts before communicating? When you learn the value of ground research and observation in crafting a story, your stories will be very different. Very different indeed.

#3. Walk your Talk

Like several great leaders before him, Martin Luther King, Jr. did not just talk. He took time to walk his talk. During the American War of Independence, George Washington spent long hours in the field with his troops. During the Civil War, Abraham Lincoln walked daily to the War Department, and toured the capital on horseback. Martin Luther King, Jr. walked and marched with civil rights activists all across the country.

By walking your talk as a leader, you add a fresh insights and perspectives to your stories that no amount of research can support. Walking is learning; learning is walking.

#4. Speak in Subtle but Substantive Terms

In his speeches, he was sometimes very subtle, but equally very substantive. He did not allow any distractions to take his focus off the issues at hand. After a Nazi hater attacked him, Martin Luther King, Jr. kept his cool. Instead of pressing charges or fighting back, he used the opportunity to display his focus on what was substantive.

He said: "I am not interested in pressing charges. I am interested in changing the kind of system that produced that kind of man." That was subtle, but substantive. This teaches us to keep our stories focused, and aimed at proving the premise, and not about irrelevant issues that are not central to the thesis at hand.

#5. Make Adequate Use of Metaphors

Martin Luther King, Jr. was the master of metaphors. He used metaphors to enhance the clarity of his message. His major speeches were loaded with metaphors to convey clarity. In the mountaintop speech, he said "I've been to the mountaintop." In another speech, he urged his comrades to press on: "Press on, and keep pressing. If you can't fly, run; if you can't run, walk; if you can't walk, CRAWL."

This is sentence is loaded with metaphors and imagery: fly, run, walk and crawl make the message compelling and persuasive to dramatize the urgency of the issue at hand.

Three Ways to Apply Lessons from this Chapter

1. **Use Hooks**

   Identify seven types of hooks that you can use to draw an audience into your story. Some examples of effective hooks are questions, stunning statistics, quotations, or expert opinions.

2. **Win by Persuasion, NOT Coercion or Alienation**

   Research some ideas from Martin Luther King, Jr.'s letters to people he did not agree with.

3. **Use Metaphors**

   Create a Metaphor Bank on your desktop to collect, sort and store metaphors for use.

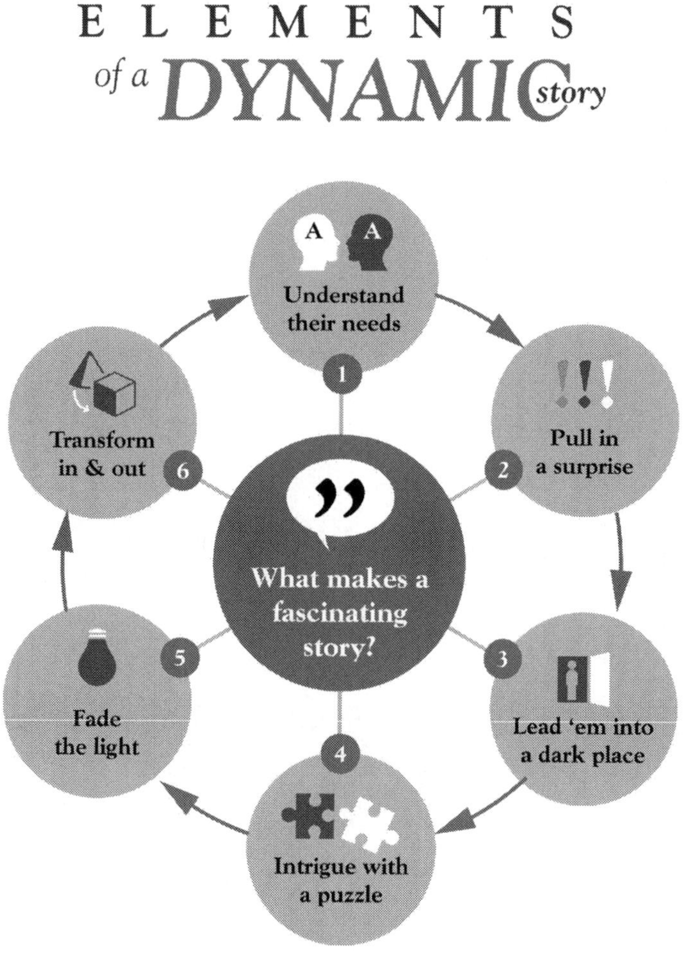

The above illustration offers some quick ideas you can infuse into your stories to keep the audience engaged at higher energy levels. The elements in this illustration come from neuroscience, the dramatic arc and my personal observation and appreciation based on several years of using stories in competitive events. Use this as a blueprint to find what works for you. The important thing is to know that storytelling is a combination of science, art and a personal mystery factor that I am yet to fully appreciate.

Epilogue

What Happens When You Win Hearts & Minds? You Get Buzz in the Marketplace

The Invisible Instrument

When used effectively, stories play the role of an invisible musical instrument that generates admiration and giggles from onlookers in the marketplace. You never know how far your story or idea will travel or resonate with your audiences. Neither can you foretell how strong the echo of your voice will reverberate in the marketplace.

When they leave, they talk about your song or rhythm to other people in the marketplace. Every storyteller has a unique voice and message. That's what makes each teller a fascinating person.

When you share your story as an experience, you are giving your audience the benefit of your own experience. They see it as a potential solution to their own challenges, not as a sale. No wonder more businesses are using this invisible instrument today to engage, communicate, and persuade. They know that if you can't engage with this invisible instrument, you can't communicate or persuade effectively.

Stories are powerful in persuading, because as invisible instruments of communication, they provide information, meaning, and entertainment. It gets the listener to tune in emotionally. When the music becomes intoxicating, we soon start nodding, humming, and sooner rather than later, tell others about the powerful experience. This is how buzz grows into news, news into prospects, prospects into leads, and leads into profit.

About the Author

Gideon F. For-mukwai is the founder of Business Storytelling Academy, formerly known as XtraMile Solutions. Prior to his entrepreneurship journey, he worked as a senior fire officer with the Singapore Civil Defense Force, fighting real fires.

Today, Gideon fights business fires, by helping emerging speakers, trainers, and entrepreneurs to capture and tell fascinating stories to generate and attract customers. As a battle-tested storyteller, he has used the craft in building his business and winning speaking awards in Singapore and USA.

For over 13 years, he has studied storytelling obsessively across 4 continents. He once drove 16 hours on two occasions to attend a storytelling workshop in Las Vegas. During the last trip, he earned himself a traffic ticket for driving a little too fast. The officer reminded him that the Nevada freeway is no Formula Race course.

Looking back at that journey and many others, Gideon believes behind every remarkable journey or fire, there is a worthwhile business lesson. He has been presenting some of those lessons to thousands of executives across the world in over 18 countries worldwide.

Wherever he goes and whatever he does, he fondly remembers that he started his journey on a pumpkin farm in the dusty fields of Africa.

Special Bonus from Gideon

Now that you have your copy of **The Science of Story Selling**, you are on your way to telling breathtaking stories! Remember this, your stories are like an invisible musical instrument that you can use to win the hearts and minds of your prospects for profit or a purpose.

You'll also receive a **special bonus** I've created for you. Add it to your bag of tools. It is what I call *Hollywood Storytelling Secrets for Business Presenters*. It is a study of the key lessons that iconic Hollywood story masters teach their clients. Hopefully, their ideas will inspire you to tell remarkable and memorable stories.

Do you want your stories to be indelible in the minds of your audiences? Start right here.

While *Hollywood Storytelling Secrets* is offered for sale, as a special bonus you can claim it for **free** here:

http://scienceofstorysellingforprofit.com/bookbonus/

The sooner you master these secrets, the better your chances for gaining more likeability and credibility that potentially leads to more profitability.

Let me know if I can be of further help.

Remember: When there is no connection, there is no persuasion,

Gideon F. For-mukwai

Made in the USA
Columbia, SC
22 December 2020

29702527R00109